A Cultural History
of the
United States

Through the Decades

The 1940s

Michael V. Uschan

Lucent Books, Inc., San Diego, California

To my niece, Megan Turner, with all my love

Library of Congress Cataloging-in-Publication Data

Uschan, Michael V., 1948-
    The 1940s / by Michael Uschan.
        p.   cm. -- (A cultural history of the United States through
    the decades)
    Includes bibliographical references (p.   ) and index.
    Summary: Discusses the political, economic, and cultural life of
one of the pivotal decades of the twentieth century, a period of
transition and crisis for the nation and for its citizens.
    ISBN 1-56006-554-0 (alk. paper)
    1. United States--History--1933-1945--Juvenile literature.
2. United States--History--1945-1953--Juvenile literature.
3. United States--Social life and customs--1918-1945--Juvenile
literature. 4. United States--Social life and customs--1945-1970-
-Juvenile literature. 5. Popular culture--United States-
-History--20th century--Juvenile literature. [1. United States-
-History--1933-1945. 2. United States--History--1945-1953.
3. United States--Social life and customs--1918-1945. 4. United
States--Social life and customs--1945-1970. 5. Popular culture-
-United States--History--20th century.] I. Title. II. Series.
E806.U63   1999
973.91--dc21   98-21005
                                                          CIP
                                                           AC

Copyright 1999 by Lucent Books, Inc.
P.O. Box 289011, San Diego, California 92198-9011

Printed in the U.S.A.

Contents

Introduction

U.S. soldiers aboard a Coast Guard landing craft prepare to land on the coast of France. World War II was the pivotal event of the forties, shaping almost everything that happened in the world and the United States in that decade.

It can be argued that the American decade of the forties actually began on December 8, 1941—the day the United States entered World War II. Until that date, Americans were still trying to resolve two major issues that had dominated the second half of the thirties. One was domestic—how to lift the United States out of the global economic disaster known as the Great Depression. The other was foreign— what role the nation should play in the armed conflicts that were raging around the world.

The Great Depression

For Americans in the '30s, "Brother, Can You Spare a Dime?" was more than a popular song. It was a reflection of the harsh reality faced by formerly productive workers who now struggled to provide food and shelter for their families. It was an acknowledgment that one thin dime could make the difference between having something to eat and going to bed hungry.

The economic boom that followed World War I came crashing to a halt on Black Tuesday, October 29, 1929, when stock market prices started to drop wildly. By the end of the year stockholders had lost more than $40 billion. This financial disaster started a chain reaction in which businesses and banks failed and millions lost their jobs.

Between 1929 and 1932 an average of 100,000 people became unemployed each week as the U.S. and world economies collapsed. At the height of this country's worst financial crisis a quarter of the nation's workers, nearly 13 million men and women, could not find jobs.

Throughout the United States were bread lines and soup kitchens, unrelenting hardship, desperation and dismay. In 1932 economist John Maynard Keynes was asked if there had ever been anything like the Great Depression. "Yes," he said, "it was called the Dark Ages and it lasted four hundred years." [1]

The New Deal

When the economy collapsed, Republican president Herbert Hoover and Congress closed what had traditionally been the strict separation of government and the nation's free

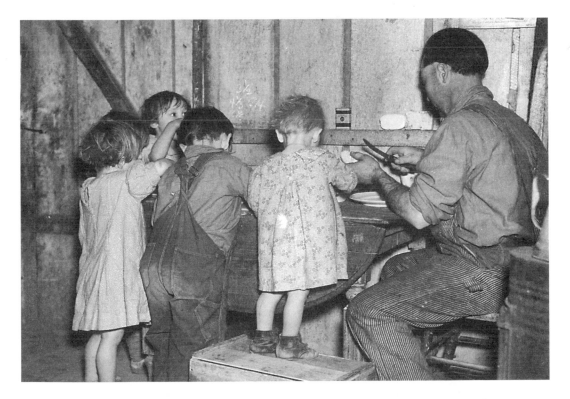

A rural family near Smithfield, Iowa, eats a sparse Christmas dinner during the Great Depression. For all too many families, there was no escape from the harsh reality of the era's poverty, even on Christmas Day.

Voters turned to President Franklin Delano Roosevelt in 1932 to rescue them from the Great Depression. The nation's longest serving president would also lead them into World War II and to the verge of victory before his death in 1945.

enterprise system, approving legislation to impose trade tariffs, stablilize banking and agriculture, and reduce mortgage foreclosures. However, the worsening worldwide depression stalled U.S. recovery, and the public grew impatient for relief.

In the 1932 presidential election, voters turned to Franklin Delano Roosevelt to rescue the nation. A member of a wealthy New York family, the popular Democratic governor of New York promised a "New Deal" of direct government aid to citizens. In his inaugural address Roosevelt reassured Americans "the only thing we have to fear is fear itself—nameless, unreasoning, unjustified terror." [2]

In a breathtaking first one hundred days in office, Roosevelt took command of the financial crisis and lifted the nation's spirits. He rammed legislation through Congress to regulate banks, provide loans to failing businesses, and create unemployment relief. By 1940 the federal government had eased the misery of Americans by spending about $16 billion on direct relief and $7 billion on public works programs.

However, it took World War II and hundreds of billions of dollars in war expenditures to lift the nation out of the Great Depression.

The Roots of World War II

By the time America entered the war, fighting had been raging for nearly a decade in the Far East, Europe, and Africa. Although Germany, Japan, and Italy—known collectively as the Axis powers—began these conflicts in the '30s, the seeds of their aggression had been sown in World War I.

The terms of the Treaty of Versailles punished Germany for starting World War I by forcing it to pay $56 billion in reparations, dismantle its military, and cede some of its most productive farmland. In addition, the Austro-Hungarian and Ottoman Empires, Germany's allies in the first global conflict, were broken up after the war and reorganized as nine new nations including Austria, Turkey, Poland, Yugoslavia, and Czechoslovakia.

The treaty crippled Germany's postwar economy and crushed the spirit of its citizens. Adolf Hitler, a spellbinding speaker and extremist politician, used this discontent to bring his National Socialist German Workers' (Nazi) Party to power in the '30s. He blamed Jews and other alleged "traitors" for losing the war. He promised to make Germany great once again and revived German dreams of expanding its borders.

Japan and Italy were both angry that their World War I allies—led by the United States, Great Britain, France, and Russia—had not rewarded them with new territory in postwar land redistribution. Their resentment helped fuel their decision to use any means necessary to gain new land and power. Thus World War I merely set the stage for more conflict.

Chapter One

Billowing smoke from the sinking USS Arizona signifies the death and destruction caused by the Japanese planes that bombed Pearl Harbor. The sneak attack pushed the United States into World War II.

America Enters the War

Although the United States played a decisive role in defeating Germany in World War I, for the next two decades, disillusioned by a bloody war that killed 116,516 of its soldiers and wounded more than 204,000, the nation reverted to its traditional foreign policy of isolationism.

This political philosophy maintained that the United States could best protect its interests by refusing to become involved with other countries. Isolationism had dominated foreign policy since 1796 when George Washington, the nation's first president, counseled the country in his farewell address to "steer clear of permanent alliances with any portion of the foreign world."[3]

After World War I the return to isolationism led the United States to refuse to join the new League of

Nations, the forerunner of today's United Nations, even though U.S. president Woodrow Wilson had originated the idea for the League and ensured its creation by making it part of the peace treaty that ended the war. Without U.S. involvement, the League quickly lost its promise, and no effective international body existed with the power to help negotiate future conflict. It was also powerless to ease underlying problems that aggravated tensions between nations, such as the worldwide depression and demands for autonomy by smaller countries and ethnic groups ruled by others.

From 1918 to 1939, many nations maneuvered to extend their power and claim more territory. There was also a new menace from Russia, which had undergone a revolution during World War I and whose Communist government now worked to subvert democratic nations to its new totalitarian doctrine. The result was that in the '30s armed conflicts began sweeping the world; conflicts that, left unchecked, would escalate into the brutal destruction of World War II.

World War II Begins

September 18, 1931, is the date most historians consider the true start of World War II. On that day Japan seized Manchuria, a province of China. Japan launched an all-out invasion of China in 1937 and by the end of the next year controlled most of its ports and industrial cities.

In 1940 Japan used the threat of military might to demand and receive concessions from Indochina, a French colony comprising modern-day Vietnam, Laos, and Kampuchea. The concessions included permission to allow Japanese military units to enter the country, which Japan would invade a year later. In 1935 Italy had conquered Ethiopia, a small country in Africa, and in 1939 invaded Albania.

But the greediest aggressor was Germany. In 1938 Hitler annexed Austria; later that year Germany seized a region of Czechoslovakia called the Sudetenland, which Hitler said rightfully belonged to Germany.

Following a policy known as appeasement, leaders in England and France tolerated both seizures of territory, naively accepting Hitler's assurances that he would be satisfied with what he had already taken. Opposition remained diplomatic in March 1939 when Germany invaded the rest of Czechoslovakia. But when Hitler's armies crossed the border into Poland on September 1, 1939, France and England finally declared war on Germany, and World War II erupted in Europe.

A motorized column of German soldiers advances through Poland. The German invasion of Poland on September 1, 1939, ignited World War II.

States refused to become directly involved in the fighting. A Roper public opinion poll in December 1939 showed 67.4 percent of Americans wanted to stay out of the conflict and did not want the United States to help either side. Americans were so convinced of the rightness of isolationism that they refused to support U.S. participation even after Hitler conquered most of Europe and Japan stepped up its military aggression in the Far East.

Isolationism Weakens

Isolationists were led by Senators Burton K. Wheeler of Montana and William E. Borah of Idaho, other congressmen, and the America First Committee, a citizens group. The committee's most famous member was Charles Lindbergh, a national hero after his historic 1927 nonstop solo flight across the Atlantic Ocean. Isolationists in the late 1930s had succeeded in passing the Neutrality Act,

Because isolationism dominated foreign policy into 1941, the United

Pearl Harbor: Why Was the United States Unprepared?

Historians blame U.S. military and political leaders for the success of the Japanese sneak attack on Pearl Harbor.

On November 27, 1941, with diplomatic talks with Japan deteriorating and the two nations seemingly on the brink of war, the War Department issued a "war warning" in the Pacific. But Adm. Husband E. Kimmel and Lt. Gen. Walter C. Short, the commanders of U.S. forces in the Pacific, failed to take adequate safeguards; they simply would not believe such an attack could happen.

The one thing Short did fear was sabotage by enemy agents. He ordered that military planes be parked together in the center of airfields to make them easier to guard. Unfortunately, neat rows of exposed aircraft were easy targets for the Japanese.

Military intelligence had broken the secret code, nicknamed Purple, that the Japanese used to transmit military and diplomatic information. By 10:30 A.M. Washington time December 7, intelligence had translated the final part of a message to Japanese diplomats. It said Japan was ending negotiations with the United States. The code breakers even knew the diplomats were ordered to deliver the message to the White House that afternoon at 1 P.M., 8 A.M. in Honolulu, the start of the Japanese attack.

War Department officials feared the message meant a Japanese military strike was about to occur, but they did not know where. Officials tried to alert Honolulu but could not get through because of poor radio reception. Instead of telephoning Kimmel or Short, they sent a Western Union telegram. It arrived in Honolulu at 7:33 A.M. Because the message was not marked urgent, a messenger on bicycle made the delivery. While he was pedaling to Pearl Harbor, the bombs began falling.

Also given too little attention was an incident involving a minesweeper on routine patrol that had spotted a midget Japanese submarine a mile and a half off Pearl Harbor at 3:42 A.M. Another U.S. ship, alerted to the threat, sank the sub with a depth charge at 6:45 A.M. But navy headquarters was not alerted to the situation for more than an hour.

Some isolationists at the time claimed U.S. officials let the attack happen because they knew it would end opposition to war, but most historians discount this theory. Rather, they point to poor decisions by a number of officials spread over several months that were all responsible for the country's greatest military disaster.

barring U.S. aid to any nation in the emerging conflicts. They vowed to keep the nation out of any foreign war.

President Roosevelt headed the interventionists, who argued that the United States must oppose the Axis powers because the conflicts begun by

Edward R. Murrow

The power of radio to affect the nation was never greater than in the live broadcasts of correspondent Edward R. Murrow from London during the Blitz.

"I'm standing on a rooftop looking out over London. At the moment everything is quiet," Murrow said in one report. "Earlier this evening we heard a number of bombs go sliding and slithering across, to fall several blocks away. Just overhead now the burst of aircraft fire. " As the planes approached, Murrow continued, "Now you'll hear two bursts a little nearer in a moment. . . . There they are! That hard, stony sound."

Listeners in America were fascinated by Murrow's descriptions of the bombing attacks. Although London was thousands of miles away, people could actually hear the roar of the attacking airplanes, the whistling of falling bombs, the booming explosions that destroyed buildings and set parts of the city on fire.

Murrow, who in the '50s became a high-profile television reporter, helped bring this distant war directly into the homes of Americans just as television news would do two decades later during the Vietnam War.

Edward R. Murrow's dramatic descriptions of the daily bombing of London in the fall of 1940 inflamed American sentiment against Germany. His live reporting was one of the most powerful uses ever of the mass medium of radio.

The moving broadcasts helped change public attitudes about World War II. They made Americans feel sympathy toward the British, which made them more willing to aid them in the war.

Germany, Italy, and Japan were really a battle between the ideologies of democracy and fascism. Interventionists saw failure to oppose Axis aggression as a threat to the free world and warned that America, as perhaps the last surviving democracy, would be left alone to fight fascism in the future. In Roosevelt's words, the U.S. would become "a lone island in a world dominated by the philosophy of force." [4]

Isolationist sentiment began to weaken in 1940 in the face of sweeping German advances. The fall of France in June, the German bombing of innocent civilians in London that summer in what became known as the Blitz, and the possibility that England might be defeated were all key factors in changing public opinion. Newspaper and radio reports about the fighting and the sympathetic portrayal of events in movies also changed public attitudes. In America, a nation of immigrants, millions of people were saddened and angered by the conquest of their former homelands. People of French, Polish, Chinese, and English heritage felt as if they, too, had been attacked by the Axis powers.

Even before Germany began conquering the rest of Europe in the spring of 1940, public sentiment in the United States had begun to shift. A May Roper poll showed 67.5 percent of Americans actively supported helping England. As German successes mounted throughout the year, isolationism continued to weaken. Its waning power was evident in Roosevelt's reelection in November to an unprecedented third term. The turnaround in public opinion made it possible for Roosevelt to start strengthening the nation's defenses and begin sending more help to beleaguered England.

In 1940 Roosevelt won congressional approval for billions of dollars for defense, responding to Roosevelt's calls for, among other things, a production capability of fifty thousand planes a year. In September Congress initiated a massive buildup of the armed forces by authorizing the first peacetime draft in history. Polls showed 71 percent of Americans supported the move. That month the president also concluded a deal with England in which the United States swapped fifty old military ships, no longer in use, for naval and air bases on British soil.

But with England under siege, Roosevelt felt the nation needed to do more. In a radio address to the nation on December 29, the president said: "The experience of the past two years has proven beyond doubt that no nation can appease the Nazis. No man can tame a tiger into a kitten by stroking it. There can be no reasoning with an incendiary bomb. . . . We must be the great arsenal of democracy." [5]

In his annual budget submitted in January 1941 Roosevelt requested a record $17.5 billion, almost 60 percent earmarked for defense spending. Its key provision was the Lend-Lease Act, which would allow the United States to finance military aid to nations fighting the Axis powers. Despite opposition by isolationists—

Wheeler opposed the bill, saying it would "plow under every fourth American boy"[6] by permitting U.S. involvement in the fighting— Congress approved lend-lease in March. The mood of the nation had changed; 70 percent of people polled now favored aid to Britain, even at the risk of war.

Lend-lease was one of the most important measures of the war. It allowed the United States to sell or give armaments to any country whose defense was considered vital to the defense of the United States. Lend-lease provided nearly $50 billion in military and economic aid to thirty-eight different nations during the war, primarily Great Britian and Russia, its principal allies.

As the United States stepped up aid to England, German submarines in 1941 began to sink scores of merchant ships ferrying supplies to Europe. When the United States began providing military convoys to protect the ships, German submarines began targeting military ships as well. The destroyer *Reuben James* was sunk on October 31 with the loss of 115 lives. In response Roosevelt issued orders permitting military vessels to shoot back when attacked.

In addition to worries over Germany, relations with Japan had deteriorated since mid-1940, when the United States quit selling oil to Japan after it threatened to invade Indochina, a French colony in Southeast Asia. When Japan did invade Indochina in July 1941, the United States responded by freezing Japanese-owned assets and refusing to sell Japan war matériel such as scrap metal. The economic sanctions hurt the Japanese, who demanded they be lifted. The United States, in turn, called for Japanese withdrawal from China and Indochina. Thus, America proceeded down the path to war against both Germany and Japan in a series of incremental steps.

Day of Infamy

The sun rose slowly over the eastern Pacific Ocean, spreading its golden warmth over the lush green mountains and sandy beaches of Oahu, the main island in the American possession of Hawaii.

People were eating breakfast, getting ready for church, pursuing other normal Sunday morning activities. From beaches and small harbors, fishing boats were heading out to sea, surfers were paddling their boards to catch the first waves of the day. At Pearl Harbor, the U.S. Pacific Fleet rocked peacefully in the gentle waves of its home port. Thousands of sailors

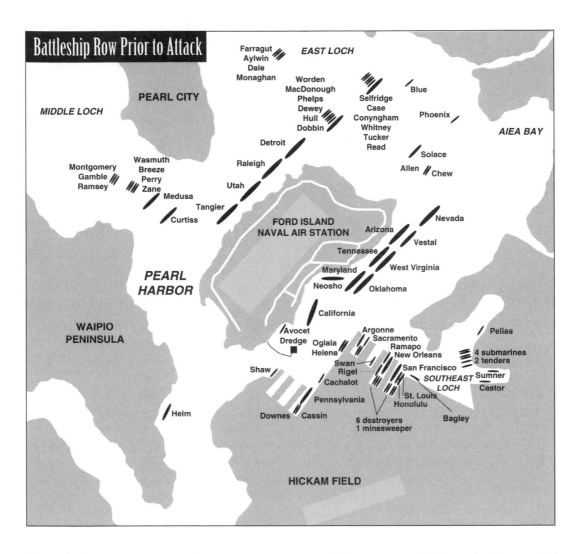

Battleship Row Prior to Attack

EAST LOCH

Farragut
Aylwin
Dale
Monaghan

Worden
MacDonough
Phelps
Dewey
Hull
Dobbin

Blue

Selfridge
Case
Conyngham
Whitney
Tucker
Read

PEARL CITY

MIDDLE LOCH

Phoenix

AIEA BAY

Detroit

Raleigh

Wasmuth
Breeze
Perry
Zane

Solace

Montgomery
Gamble
Ramsey

Allen
Chew

Utah

Medusa

Tangier

Curtiss

FORD ISLAND
NAVAL AIR STATION

Nevada

Arizona

Vestal

Tennessee

West Virginia

PEARL
HARBOR

Maryland

Neosho

Oklahoma

California

WAIPIO
PENINSULA

Avocet
Dredge
Oglala
Helena

Argonne
Sacramento
Ramapo
New Orleans

Pelias

4 submarines
2 tenders

Swan
Rigel
Cachalot

Shaw

San Francisco

SOUTHEAST
LOCH

Sumner

Castor

Pennsylvania

St. Louis
Honolulu

Downes
Cassin

6 destroyers
1 minesweeper

Bagley

Helm

HICKAM FIELD

aboard ship were just waking up to a relaxed day of duty.

But at 7:55 A.M., the tranquil beauty of this paradise of the Pacific was shattered by one of the most daring and treacherous acts of military might the world had ever seen. It was Sunday, December 7, 1941, a turning point in U.S. history.

A Japanese task force had traveled undetected to within 220 miles of Oahu. Its mission was to cripple the U.S. Navy so Japanese military conquest in the Far East and the Pacific could continue unchallenged. Launched from aircraft carriers, 350 planes roared down in two waves from the green-clad mountains of the

Franklin Delano Roosevelt

Franklin Delano Roosevelt, who guided the nation out of the Great Depression and led it to victory in World War II, is considered one of the greatest presidents in U.S. history.

Roosevelt is the only chief executive to serve more than two terms. He was president for slightly more than twelve years before his death on April 12, 1945, just weeks before the German surrender.

President Franklin D. Roosevelt talks to Americans in one of his many radio addresses, which became known as "fireside chats." Roosevelt used radio more effectively than any previous public figure had.

Isolationists branded Roosevelt the nation's "No. 1 warmonger" because he led the fight to strengthen the armed forces and to become involved in the spreading world conflict. As early as 1937 he warned that if fascist aggression was left unchecked, "Let no one imagine that America will escape . . . that this Western Hemisphere will not be attacked." Roosevelt risked unpopularity with his interventionist convictions. He feared that if nothing was done to stop Germany and Japan, the United States would be at their mercy in the future.

A distant cousin of President Theodore Roosevelt, FDR dedicated his life to public service. He was an assistant secretary of the navy, New York state senator, and New York governor before being elected president for the first time in 1932. He was reelected in 1936, 1940, and 1944.

In 1921 Roosevelt contracted polio, which left him permanently crippled and dependent on metal leg braces and crutches but did not deter him from a political career. Because of his energy, intelligence, and dynamic personality, as well as the minimizing of his disability by cooperative media, his fitness for high office was rarely questioned.

Roosevelt was a shrewd politician and the first president able to exploit the new mass medium of radio. Radio became a powerful tool for Roosevelt to communicate directly with citizens and to win their support on important issues. An eloquent speaker, Roosevelt held many radio news conferences and delivered informal addresses to the public. In these "fireside chats," as they were called, the president would talk plainly and simply to Americans about problems facing the nation.

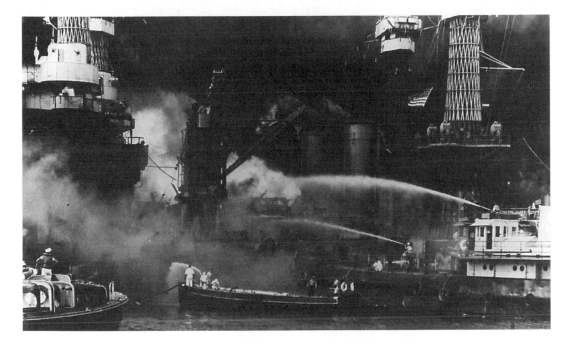

Sailors attempt to extinguish flames engulfing the USS West Virginia.
Although the attack on Pearl Harbor caught them by surprise, American fighting men fought valiantly and worked heroically to save their comrades.

Koolau Range, striking with deadly fury at Pearl Harbor and the Wheeler and Hickam airfields. Surprised sailors and flight crews at first thought the planes might be their own. Then they saw the round red markings on each plane, the rising sun symbol of Japan.

Japanese planes flew low, launching torpedoes that surged through the water and exploded in the midsections of U.S. ships. The attackers dropped bombs to destroy planes that were parked neatly in rows. Gunners fired at other targets on the ground,

including military personnel running madly to seek cover or get to their fighting stations.

Sailors and soldiers bravely tried to fight back. One of them was Dorie Miller, a twenty-two-year-old black sailor from Waco, Texas, who was a mess attendant on the USS *West Virginia.* Awakened by the first of six torpedoes that struck his ship, Miller went topside to fight.

Miller helped move wounded personnel to safety and then manned an unattended machine gun. He downed

The event proclaimed on the the headline of the newspaper this young boy is trying to sell not only angered Americans, it scared them. For weeks after Pearl Harbor, people all over America feared Japan or its ally Germany were preparing to strike somewhere else in the United States.

four planes before heat and flames from the burning ship forced him to leap into the ocean. Miller received the Navy Cross for his heroism. He died on Thanksgiving Day 1943 when his new ship, an aircraft carrier, was sunk during a sea battle.

Less than two hours after it had begun, the attack was over and Pearl Harbor was a smoking, blazing mili-

tary junkyard. The Japanese sank or seriously damaged 18 ships, 8 of them battleships, destroyed 188 planes, killed 2,403 people, and wounded 1,178. They also launched America into World War II.

The Nation Unites for War

The next day, in stirring words, President Franklin D. Roosevelt asked Congress to declare war on Japan:

Yesterday, December 7, 1941—a date which will live in infamy—the United States was suddenly and deliberately attacked by the naval and air forces of the empire of Japan. . . . With confidence in our armed forces—with the unbounded determination of our people—we will help gain the inevitable triumph—so help us God. [7]

Within an hour the Senate voted unanimously to declare war on Japan, and the House quickly concurred. The only no vote was cast by Representative Jeannette Rankin, a pacifist from Montana, who had also voted against fighting in World War I. Both of Rankin's no votes cost her her seat in the following elections.

But Rankin was one of only a handful of people left in the entire nation who did not want war. *New York Times* columnist Arthur Krock wrote that the new prowar unity was so strong, so universal that "you could almost hear it click into place." Even isolationist leader Wheeler declared: "The only thing now to do is to lick the hell out of them." [8]

Pearl Harbor Panic Sweeps the Nation

After Pearl Harbor, many Americans thought that an all-out attack on the United States was inevitable.

The next day Lt. Gen. John L. DeWitt, chief of West Coast defense, said, "This is war. Death and destruction may come at any moment." [9] Although hysterical claims like his proved groundless, Americans believed Japan and Germany were preparing to bomb them. For the first time since the War of 1812, the United States feared invasion.

In the first few weeks following the sneak attack, mistaken sightings of "enemy planes" touched off air raid warnings in major cities. The fear was greatest on the West Coast, where the military built machine-gun fortifications on beaches to repel an expected Japanese invasion. In New York, Mayor Fiorello LaGuardia predicted, "The war will come right to our cities and residential districts." [10] The senior officer of the Wisconsin American Legion asked twenty-five thousand licensed deer hunters to volunteer for a militia to fight enemy soldiers. Washington, D.C., the nation's capital, became an armed fortress. Machine guns were mounted on the roof of the White House and a plane was kept warmed up at a nearby airfield to evacuate the president in case of attack.

Throughout the nation people draped heavy cloth over their windows (blackout curtains) so no light would escape to give enemy planes a target. Searchlights and volunteer spotters scanned the night skies in search of attacking planes.

Except for a few minor incidents, the war never reached the United States. But the anger, fear, and hatred Pearl Harbor generated united Americans more strongly than at any other time in history.

Gearing Up for War

When America entered the war it faced two major challenges: to dramatically increase its military strength and to rapidly implement a wartime economy. This meant retooling businesses and industries to produce planes, tanks, ships, airplanes, bullets, bombs, and other war matériel.

Uncle Sam rolls up his sleeve and gets ready to fight in World War II.
The real message of this patriotic poster, however, was that the nation
was calling on its young men to enlist and help their country win the war.

The manpower problem was easily solved. In December 1941 the army had only 1.6 million soldiers and the navy only a few hundred thousand. But Pearl Harbor sent a shock wave of patriotism through the nation. In just a few days thousands of young men took up the battle cry "Remember Pearl Harbor!" and flooded army and navy recruiting stations. By the end of the war voluntary enlistment and the draft had placed more than 15.1 million men and women in uniform—10.4 million army (which included the

air force), 3.9 million navy, 600,000 marines, and 250,000 Coast Guard.

But despite the heroism and efficiency of its armed forces, America's greatest weapon was its industrial might. The nation's productive capacity was larger than that of all Axis countries combined. Even Japanese admiral Isoroku Yamamoto, commander of the Japanese navy, feared this American strength. He once cautioned his nation's leaders: "Do not forget American industry is much more developed than ours—and unlike us,

How Movies Shaped Prewar Attitudes

The 1941 film *Sergeant York* tells the story of Alvin York, a young pacifist from rural Tennessee who at first resists the draft, but finally decides World War I is a just war and becomes his country's greatest hero. Gary Cooper not only won an Academy Award for best actor for his portrayal of York, but also may have helped make his country more willing to fight in World War II.

In the three years before Pearl Harbor, Hollywood produced about fifty movies with an anti-Nazi theme. These included *Confessions of a Nazi Spy* (1939), starring Edward G. Robinson as an FBI agent who tracks down Nazi spies, and *The Great Dictator* (1940), a satire in which silent movie great Charlie Chaplin plays both a barber in a Jewish ghetto and a dictator who is a dead ringer for Adolf Hitler.

Isolationists claimed movies like these and *Sergeant York* were prowar propaganda. In mid-1941 a U.S. Senate subcommittee chaired by isolationist Gerald P. Nye of South Dakota investigated this alleged movie bias. Nye opened the hearings by saying it was wrong that people went to films like *Sergeant York* expecting to be entertained and instead had to "listen to a speech designed to make you believe that Hitler is going to get you."

Wendell Willkie, the losing Republican candidate in the 1940 presidential election, defended the movie industry. "If you charge that the motion picture industry as a whole and its leading executives as individuals are opposed to the Nazi dictatorship in Germany . . . there need be no investigation," Willkie said. "We abhor everything Hitler represents."

The hearings adjourned on September 26; the subcommittee never issued a report because the attack on Pearl Harbor made the issue irrelevant.

they have all the oil they want. Japan cannot beat America. Therefore, she should not fight America."[11]

As it had done in World War I, the U.S. government took direct control of the nation's economy. The War Powers Act, passed two weeks after Pearl Harbor, gave the president extraordinary powers to manage the nation's industrial might.

The federal government had the power to allocate raw materials, establish priorities for production, and ration supplies and output. The government told businesses what to make, set quotas, and could take over plants if production quotas were not met. It even had the power to allocate workers to specific industries.

President Roosevelt and Congress established the War Production Board (WPB), Office of Price Administration (OPA), Office of Economic Stability (OES), and a host of other governmental agencies to guide the war

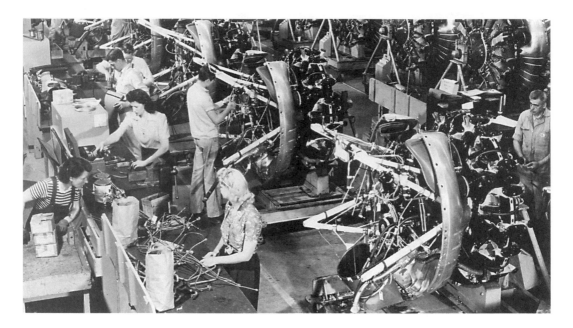

Workers in this Douglas aircraft plant in August 1943 are making SBD Dauntless dive-bomber engines. Workers on the home front provided the weapons and material American soldiers and sailors needed to win the war.

economy. OPA controlled prices, including rent, to forestall the inflation that had plagued the nation during World War I.

The automobile industry is a good example of the conversion of the national economy to a war footing. The government simply told auto companies they could no longer make cars. For the rest of the war their plants manufactured tanks, planes, and other military supplies.

It was a complete reversal of the free enterprise system that had made America great, but there were few complaints because defense industries were allowed to make money—overall corporate profits rose from $5 billion in 1939 to $10.8 billion in 1944. The war created 17 million new jobs and boosted industrial production by 96 percent.

Congress began to fund war production by appropriating $100 billion during the first six months of 1942 and another $60 billion before the year was over. The United States also approved loans to Allied nations such as Great Britain, which bought even more weapons and supplies from

American companies. Estimates of the total costs of the war were near $330 billion; at its peak in 1943 war spending amounted to an amazing $190,000 per second.

From July 1940 to the end of the war in August 1945, American factories and shipyards produced almost 300,000 military planes, 86,000 tanks, 8.5 million rifles and carbines, 3 million machine guns, 72,000 naval ships, 4,900 merchant ships to carry vital supplies to the Allies, and 14 million tons of ammunition and explosives.

U.S. industries set records for production of oil, steel, aluminum, and other essential raw materials. The nation's agricultural resources were another important weapon. In addition to feeding its civilian population and U.S. forces scattered around the world, American farmers helped feed Allied soldiers and civilians and the growing population of war refugees. Though the number of farm dwellers declined by 17 percent from 1940 to 1945, farm production increased by more than 25 percent due to mechanization and consolidation of smaller farms. In that same period farm income more than tripled to $9.5 billion.

Every American Had to Fight

It took the tragedy of Pearl Harbor to awaken the nation from its isolationist slumber, but once aroused, Americans proved worthy of the task that faced them. Millions of men and women willingly went to far-off places to fight, and sometimes die, for their homeland.

But victory in World War II came not only from the heroics of its armed forces, but also from the countless daily sacrifices made by American civilians of all ages. They manufactured the weapons soldiers needed to fight, grew food to feed them, raised money to fund the war, and provided an outpouring of love that helped sustain soldiers and sailors during the fighting.

The United States was the home front, a battleground that was no less important than the front lines of Europe and the Pacific. The home front—where average people devoted extraordinary effort to the cause of victory; where everyone from young children to senior citizens had to make sacrifices for victory; where tens of millions of people put in endless hours of hard work and drudgery.

Chapter Two

Women workers apply fixtures to the fuselage of a B-17 bomber. With millions of men in the military, women were needed to work in plants, factories, and at scores of other jobs that had traditionally been held by men.

America at War: The Home Front

In a radio address the day after the United States declared war on Japan, President Roosevelt told civilians that, like the soldiers who would do the fighting, they too had "a grave responsibility to the nation now and for the duration of this war." [12] The phrase "for the duration" came to symbolize the many sacrifices average Americans would have to make.

During World War II, average Americans believed that the home front—the United States—was simply another battleground in the war. They sacrificed in many ways, putting up with restrictive government regulations, making donations to wartime charities, and working long hours to produce the weapons needed to defeat the enemy.

Shoppers wait patiently in line to buy sugar, one of the many items rationed during World War II. Civilians endured long lines and shortages of meat, sugar, and other scarce commodities during the war.

The two most obvious sacrifices these soldiers of the home front endured were shortages of consumer products and rationing. The war machine devoured petroleum, steel, rubber tires, wool, and other vital raw material as well as meat, butter, coffee, animal fats, and other foods. Although the United States was the world's largest agricultural producer, food was rationed because the nation had to feed Allied soldiers and victims of the war in Europe as well as its own soldiers and civilians.

Thus, World War II changed the daily lives of every man, woman, and child in America in a variety of ways.

It affected what they ate, what they wore, where they lived, their family lives, and even where they were free to travel.

War Changes Daily Life

The war altered people's diets because of the need to conserve scarce foods such as meat and sugar. Rationing made shopping difficult and time-consuming. Americans needed ration coupons to purchase foods; even if they had the coupon for meat, however, that didn't mean meat was in stock in local markets. The scarcity of some items made cooking difficult, although countless creative cooks altered stan-

Rationing

Rationing was confusing, complicated, and just plain exasperating—the most difficult wartime problem civilians had to deal with on a daily basis.

The average gasoline ration was three gallons a week; the yearly butter ration twelve pounds per person, 25 percent less than normal; the yearly limit for canned goods thirty-three pounds, thirteen pounds under usual consumption levels; and people could buy only three new pairs of shoes a year.

The Office of Price Administration issued ration stamps that authorized people to buy scarce items. When people used up their stamps for meat or gasoline, they were out of luck. The stamps became more important than the money needed to pay for such items.

Ration stamps themselves could be confusing, for store owners as well as for shoppers. Stamps for food came in two colors—red for meat, cheese, and fats, and blue for processed foods. Shoppers had to make sure to take the right ones to the store.

Stamps also had point values, which made for difficult decisions. A person

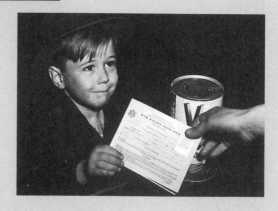

This young boy needed ration stamps as well as money to make this purchase. Rationing was a frustrating, confusing part of daily life for Americans during World War II.

buying meat who had 12 points could use them all on a single pound of round steak. Or the shopper could purchase a greater quantity of another meat, such as hamburger which was valued at only 7 points a pound.

Even when people had the proper stamps, stores were often out of what they wanted. When scarce items were in stock, crowds quickly cleared the shelves.

dard recipes to make do. The scarcity of meat, for example, led to substitution of oats and other grains and meal to make "meatless sausage" and other meatless dishes. Food shortages also made going out to dinner something of an adventure, as patrons could never be sure what menu items restaurants could offer.

Artificial sweeteners, used in place

of sugar, affected the taste of chocolate and candy, making sweets less appealing. People conserved coffee by reusing grounds again and again, producing an increasingly unpalatable, watery brew nicknamed "Roosevelt coffee." Butter was very scarce, replaced by vegetable margarine called oleo. In the past, most people had rejected this cheaper alternative to butter because it did not taste as good. Now they had no choice. Because oleo was white when produced, it was usually sold with a packet of yellow coloring that could be mixed in by hand to make it at least look more like butter.

To counter food shortages Americans planted "victory gardens," as people had done in World War I. City dwellers grew tomatoes, onions, corn, and other vegetables in plots in their yards, along grassy boulevards, and even in wooden boxes outside apartment windows. In 1943 more than 20 million gardens produced almost one-third of the vegetables Americans consumed that year. Urban families also raised chickens and rabbits for meat in small coops and hutches around the country.

Americans have always been a people who prized their freedom to travel wherever and whenever they wanted. But wartime restrictions reduced travel opportunities for average citizens. Rationing of gasoline and tires meant that driving was curtailed; reduced "victory" speed limits that conserved gas and tires meant trips took longer. Ride sharing became popular and people jammed buses and other mass transportation.

Railroads, the main form of long-distance transportation, were crowded with troops and military shipments, and civilians holding train tickets could be bumped by military personnel.

Black Market

There was one place to shop during World War II where shortages and rationing did not exist: the black market.

The term *black market* refers to any type of illegal sales. A Gallup poll during the war showed that one in four Americans condoned at least an occasional visit to "Mr. Black," as underground dealers were known. It is estimated that such transactions involved more than 25 percent of all retail business during the war and were worth about $1 billion a year.

Some black market sales no doubt involved stolen goods. But most black market transactions were by merchants who wanted to help a friend or special customer buy hard-to-get items. It was just a way of rewarding good customers.

Some black marketers sold scarce items at inflated prices. A pound of boneless ham might cost $1.25, nearly double the regular price, and a pair of nylon stockings, one of the most prized wartime possessions, might be an astronomical $5.

Black market goods were so abundant that an investigative reporter for a Pittsburgh newspaper was able to buy a ton of meat for $2,000. He did not need any ration stamps to make the purchase.

The Domestic War

For the most part World War II bypassed U.S. soil. There was no West Coast invasion, but the Japanese did manage a few insignificant attacks.

On February 23, 1942, a submarine surfaced off the coast of Santa Barbara, California, and fired twenty-five shells at an oil refinery. Some shells landed a mile inland but did little damage. The only bombing occurred September 29, 1942, when two incendiary bombs were dropped on a forest region in Oregon. The resulting fire was soon put out. The plane had been carried across the Pacific Ocean in a Japanese submarine and launched by catapult.

In 1944 and 1945 Japan attacked the West Coast, mostly unsuccessfully, with thousands of large paper balloons carrying thirty-pound bombs. Built by schoolchildren, they were released in Japan and rode air currents to the United States. About three hundred are believed to have fallen in Canada and the United States, drifting as far inland as Iowa and Kansas. Most did little or no damage but one landed on Oregon's Mount Gearhart, killing six people — the only deaths on the mainland due to enemy action.

Some civilians were killed accidentally during the war by U.S. military personnel. Sixty-eight people died when navy artillery shells fired during the attack on Pearl Harbor fell in the city of Honolulu. And on August 10, 1944, a military plane on a night training mission accidentally dropped bombs on a farm in Florida. Four members of a family were killed and a fifth was left paralyzed.

Clothing styles were to a great extent dictated by necessity, as well. Because wool was needed for uniforms, men's suits no longer came with the traditional second pair of pants. Also out were vests and trouser cuffs. The government mandated that women's hemlines could be no longer than an inch above the knee and reduced the cloth in women's swimwear by 10 percent. "The two-piece bathing suit," noted the *Wall Street Journal* in 1942, "now is tied in with the war as closely as the zipperless dress and the pleatless skirt."[13] (Pleats were banned to conserve cloth.)

Nylon and silk were needed to make parachutes, creating a shortage of sheer stockings. Some women camouflaged their lack of stylish hosiery by painting a seam up the back of their legs or applying dark makeup. Liquid leg makeup was sometimes called "bottled stockings." Some women tried to rent nylons for important occasions by advertising in newspapers.

Finding a place to live, maybe even a rented room in which to sleep between work shifts, was a major problem for many people during the war. A severe housing shortage was created because millions of people moved to different areas of the country to find work and because no new homes were being built. By the end of 1945 more than 15 million civilians lived in a county different from their county of residence before Pearl Harbor.

The housing problem was most severe in California and major cities in the northeast, areas where new defense industries were concentrated and which were flooded with new residents. For example, the small northern Illinois community of Seneca had 1,250 residents in 1940. When the government opened a defense plant to make landing craft for the navy, Seneca's population ballooned overnight by 500 percent. Washington, D.C., also became overcrowded because of the influx of tens of thousands of new federal workers and thousands of military personnel. In some cities workers shared "hot beds" in rooming houses, renting them for eight-hour sleeping shifts.

Defense Workers

Ironically, the jobs created by the war gave people money to spend for the first time in years, but rationing and shortages made it impossible to buy the things they wanted. New jobs in defense industries reduced unemploy-

This poster from the War Production Co-ordinating Committee encourages women to become a vital part of the war effort. Women responded to the challenge, with 7 million of them joining the workforce during the war.

ment from 9 million in 1940 to less than 1 million by the end of 1942. Workers also drew higher wages, with weekly earnings in manufacturing rising from $25 in 1940 to $45.70 in 1944. The average workweek was nine hours a day, six days a week, with plenty of overtime.

Because so many men were away fighting, industries faced labor short-

This riveter at the Lockheed Aircraft Corporation is just one of the hundreds of thousands of women who worked in the nation's factories during World War II. These industrious women made the planes and tanks that their husbands, brothers, and sons used to win the war.

ages. The solution was to increase the hiring of women. The number of women workers rose from 12 million in 1940 to 19 million five years later, accounting for nearly a third of all workers. By the end of the war some factories employed more women than men.

Symbolized by the fictional "Rosie the Riveter," women workers helped make the planes, tanks, ships, and guns that won the war. Women also took other traditionally male jobs as miners, meatpackers, cab drivers,

lumberjacks, welders, and railroad workers. This is how Lila Morgan of Pratt, Kansas, described her transition to war worker: "After I graduated from high school, I traded in my poodle skirts and saddle oxfords for denim pants and steel-toed shoes. As a production clerk in a munitions plant, I was helping our troops win the war. At 18, I was making as much money as my father, who'd been working for a refinery for 25 years." [14]

Women workers began wearing slacks to work, setting a fashion trend for the entire nation. Most wore kerchiefs to keep their hair out of the way of machinery or cut their hair shorter. To encourage women to wear safer hairstyles, the defense industries asked popular actress Veronica Lake to change her hairstyle. Lake's trademark long blond hair hung down over her face and covered one eye. Patriotically, Lake did her part for the war effort by cutting her hair shorter.

As they had during World War I, about 700,000 blacks left southern states to find work and a better way of life in northern cities. Until the war most blacks were restricted to menial jobs as janitors, waiters, maids, and bellhops. Even when war production began to expand in 1940, some defense industries refused to hire blacks. But when black leaders vowed to march on Washington on July 1, 1941, President Roosevelt responded by issuing an executive order on racial equality. The order created the Fair Employment Practices Commission and prohibited discrimination in defense industries. This opened the way for hundreds of thousands of black workers to find good jobs. But even in the north, blacks, who in 1940 made up about 10 percent of the nation's population, had to live in seg-regated areas and were barred from some restaurants and hotels.

Japanese Americans

The group of Americans treated most unjustly during the war were of Japanese decent. In early 1942 the government rounded up 110,000 Japanese living on the West Coast and moved them to ten internment camps, called relocation centers, in California, Arizona, Idaho, Utah, Wyoming, and Arkansas. Men, women, and children, most of them American citizens, were forced to live in poorly constructed tar paper shacks in camps patrolled by armed soldiers. Japanese Americans

The Mochida family awaits evacuation by bus to a Japanese internment camp; note that the children are wearing ID tags so they will not be separated from their families. The internment of Japanese citizens was a terrible abuse of their civil rights—one the nation came to regret when the war was over.

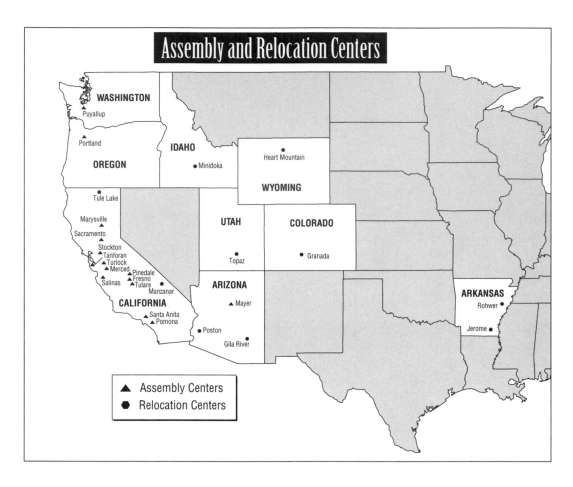

Assembly and Relocation Centers

WASHINGTON
▲ Puyallup

▲ Portland

OREGON

IDAHO

● Minidoka

● Heart Mountain

WYOMING

▲ Tule Lake

Marysville ▲

Sacramento ▲

Stockton ▲
▲ Tanforan
▲ Turlock
▲ Merced ● Pinedale
Salinas ▲ ▲ Fresno
● ▲ Tulare
● Manzanar

CALIFORNIA

▲ Santa Anita
▲ Pomona

● Poston

Gila River ●

UTAH

● Topaz

COLORADO

● Granada

ARIZONA

▲ Mayer

ARKANSAS
Rohwer ●

Jerome ●

▲ Assembly Centers
● Relocation Centers

living in Hawaii, where they made up one-third of the population, were not forced into internment camps.

The government defended internment as in the interest of national security, claiming that Japanese Americans would help soldiers from their former homeland if Japan invaded the West Coast. But during the war there was not one incident in which a Japanese American aided the enemy in any way. Although any Japanese living in the United States was considered a threat, only a few thousand residents of German or Italian descent were imprisoned, and then only if a government investigation determined they were actual security risks.

The United States denied the civil rights of internees simply because they were Japanese. Even Milton Eisenhower, one of the officials in charge of the relocation, questioned the decision: "When this war is over, I feel most deeply that we as Americans are going to regret the avoidable injustices of this unprecedented migration." [15]

By late 1943 about thirty thousand internees were allowed to leave the camps to work. About fifteen hundred enlisted and nearly eight thousand Japanese Americans served in the armed forces during the war, often with great distinction.

In late 1944 the U.S. Supreme Court ruled the internment had been unconstitutional and the Japanese were freed. Because many internees had lost thousands of dollars in property when they were forced to relocate, Congress in 1948 granted individuals indemnities of up to $2,500. In 1988 the federal government issued a formal apology for the internment of Japanese Americans and gave survivors $20,000 each. The apology and indemnity were initiated in a bill in 1980 by Representative Norman Mineta of California and Senator Daniel Inouye of Hawaii, who lost an arm fighting during World War II.

Family Life

World War II severely and adversely affected the quality of traditional family life. Family members feared daily for the lives of loved ones who were away fighting. The death, injury, or capture of sons, daughters, and spouses took a terrible toll on families.

Many women became the heads of their families, often assuming new, sometimes frightening responsibilities while taking jobs outside the home for the first time. One of the effects of family disruption was a decline in adult supervision of children because so many parents were away fighting or working. Parents just weren't around as much as they had been in the past. The problem was compounded by a lack of child-care facilities. The term "latchkey child" was used for the first time to refer to children, also called "eight-hour orphans," who went home after school to empty homes,

Lack of parental supervision was blamed, in part, for increased juvenile delinquency. In 1942 juvenile arrests nationwide climbed 17 percent from a year earlier. Juvenile delinquency was a problem during the entire war. In San Diego, California, site of a large naval base, the arrest rate for boys in 1943 rose 55 percent from a year earlier and for girls skyrocketed 355 percent. Many teenage girls got into trouble because they flocked to areas where servicemen could be found. They dated soldiers and sailors out of a misplaced sense of patriotism and because it made them feel grown-up.

Wartime Sports

Although professional sports continued to be very popular during World War II, the caliber of play nosedived because so many athletes went to war. Baseball, the nation's most popular sport, was hit especially hard as one thousand players went into the service, including Ted Williams and Hank Greenberg, the game's highest paid player in 1941 at $55,000 a year.

Wartime desperation for players led the Cincinnati Reds in 1944 to sign Joe Nuxhall, a fifteen-year-old pitcher, and the same year the Brooklyn Dodgers had a half-dozen players over forty. The St. Louis Browns in 1945 even fielded Pete Gray, who had lost his left arm in an auto accident as a child.

The National Football League (NFL) lost so many players (638) that in 1944 the Chicago Cardinals and Pittsburgh Steelers merged for one season as the Card-Pitts. George Halas, owner-coach of the Chicago Bears, became a lieutenant commander in the navy.

College sports suffered because of a lack of student athletes and travel restrictions. There was also the oddity of the 1941 Rose Bowl being moved three thousand miles east from Pasadena, California, to Durham, North Carolina. Played just a few weeks after Pearl Harbor, officials had feared a West Coast attack by Japan. (Oregon State beat Duke 20–16.)

Boxing remained a big draw despite the loss of its greatest star, Joe Louis, who had defended his heavyweight title one last time in 1942 before entering the army. After he knocked out Buddy Baer in the first round, he donated his purse to the Navy Relief Fund. Louis spent the war entertaining troops with boxing exhibitions.

Baseball and football players also toured military camps to boost morale. St. Louis Cardinals star Enos Slaughter once played an exhibition baseball game on Iwo Jima.

World War II created new families as couples rushed into marriage, some because they feared they would never see one another again. Some men got married to avoid being drafted. When the draft was being considered in 1940, the national marriage rate rose dramatically from 9.6 per thousand in May to 14.7 in September, the month Congress passed the Selective Service Act. Some young couples rushed to have children for the same reason, although later in the war even fathers were drafted.

The Volunteer Spirit: From War Bonds to Scrap Drives

The war brought out the volunteer spirit in millions of Americans. They rolled bandages for soldiers; collected vital resources like scrap metal, rubber, and other scarce material; helped entertain troops; and bought and helped sell war bonds.

The Office of Civilian Defense organized about 19 million volunteers into a nationwide network of civil defense wardens. Wearing white metal helmets and armbands and carrying gas masks, they patrolled neighborhood streets during emergency drills. Volunteers also helped the national Aircraft Warning Service scan the skies for enemy planes.

In 1944 alone patriotic citizens collected 7 millions tons of wastepaper, 84,807 tons of fats, 18.5 million tons of iron and steel scrap, 185,676 tons of tin cans, and 544,739 tons of rags, all listed as needed for the war effort. Children were heavily involved in scrap drives and schools often served as collection centers. They even donated dolls and other toys made of rubber.

Paper might not seem important to winning a war. But in 1944 the army and navy used a billion paper food containers and it took nearly eleven hundred square feet of paper packing to wrap a single P-51 Mustang airplane for shipping. The bundles of scrap paper children collected and hauled in their wagons helped make this possible.

Other patriotic efforts included the selling of war bonds. To help pay for the $330 billion cost of the war, citizens purchased $135 billion in war

Movie star Rita Hayworth shows other Americans she has sacrificed her car's metal bumpers for the war effort. The government showcased celebrities like Hayworth to inspire other Americans to make similar sacrifices.

bonds in denominations from $25 to $10,000

Celebrities helped by starring in war bond rallies. Carole Lombard, a Hollywood star and the wife of actor Clark Gable, appeared in the first rally January 12, 1942, in Indianapolis. "Heads up, hands up, America!" she told a crowd of three thousand. "Let's give a cheer that will be heard in Tokyo and Berlin."[16] Lombard autographed every bond, helping sell bonds worth more than $2 million in

The V-Home Pledge

A pamphlet distributed in 1942 by the Office of Civilian Defense shows the kind of sacrifices expected of average American families to help win the war.

The document began by praising Americans for doing their bit by "making millions of small sacrifices," then detailed the kind of activities valued most highly: "They are saving and salvaging, conserving and converting. They are foregoing small pleasures, putting up with inconveniences and annoyances. They are doing these things freely and gladly because they understand the meaning of the fight for freedom: freedom for themselves, their children, and the America they love."

The pamphlet included the following V-Home (Victory Home) Pledge, which laid down guidelines for patriotic wartime behavior (italics are from the original):

I. *This home follows the instructions of its air-raid warden,* in order to protect itself against attack by air.

II. This home *conserves* food, clothing, transportation, and health, in order to hasten an unceasing flow of war materials to our men at the front.

III. This home *salvages* essential materials, in order that they may be converted to immediate war uses.

IV. This home *refuses to spread rumors* designed to divide our Nation.

V. This home *buys* War Savings Stamps and bonds *regularly.*

We are doing these things because we know we must *to Win This War.*

flight back to California. President Roosevelt awarded her a posthumous medal as the first American woman to die in action in World War II.

In schools students bought war stamps for a dime or quarter, eventually collecting enough to buy a war bond. In 1944 alone school sales of war bonds paid for 11,700 parachutes, 2,900 planes, and more than 44,000 jeeps. Students sang patriotic songs like this one, with lyrics sung to the tune of "My Bonnie Lies over the Ocean":

> Buy Jeeps, Buy Jeeps,
> Send thousand of Jeeps o'er
> the sea, the sea.
> Buy Jeeps, Buy Jeeps,
> And bring back my loved one
> to me. [17]

The USO

During the war the United Service Organizations (USO) entertained servicemen at home and overseas. Volunteers opened three thousand recreational centers called canteens, where soldiers could have a bite to eat, listen to music, and meet other young people. Also visiting USO centers were young women who had moved to new cities during the war and, like servicemen, were far from home and family.

one day. Tragically, Lombard was killed when her plane crashed on the

The Hollywood Canteen in Los Angeles was the most famous because movie stars waited on tables, served food, washed dishes, and performed. A band played every night and soldiers and sailors danced with Hedy Lamarr, Betty Grable, Joan Crawford, Marlene Dietrich, and other stars. The Hollywood Canteen could hold only one thousand at a time, so it ran five shifts a night to entertain more people.

Hundreds of actors, singers, comedians, and musicians in the USO's Camp Shows Division performed at military bases at home and overseas. Comedian Bob Hope, one of the decade's biggest stars, traveled extensively to combat areas. His troupe always included a band and some of Hollywood's most beautiful actresses.

In the three years after Pearl Harbor, more than thirty-five hundred performers made more than thirty-five thousand personal appearances to entertain soldiers. Glenn Miller, the most popular bandleader of his time, and his entire band were inducted into the army as a special unit to entertain soldiers. Another victim of the war, Miller was killed in December 1945 when his plane crashed en route from England to Paris.

The Real Heroes

Although every American on the

Comedian Bob Hope entertains troops during a 1944 USO show. He was one of many performers who volunteered to go overseas to entertain lonely American soldiers and sailors.

home front was waging war in the way he or she knew best, civilians back in the United States all knew who the real heroes were—the members of the armed forces who were fighting battles all around the world to ensure their country's safety.

Americans obsessively followed the course of the conflict; they read newspapers and magazines, tuned in to radio broadcasts, and went to movie theaters to watch newsreels of combat. People hung maps of the world in their homes and charted advances and retreats with colored pins, concern made all the more poignant when a son, daughter, spouse, or parent was fighting in that far-off place marked by a simple colored pin.

Chapter Three

These U.S. airmen return in triumph to America after helping defeat Germany. Superior U.S. and Allied air power was one of the decisive factors in winning World War II.

Winning the War

The letter from the "President of the United States" began simply enough: "Greeting. You are hereby ordered to report for induction into the Armed Forces of the United States." Draft notices transformed millions of young men into "GIs," a slang term for soldiers from the abbreviation for "government issue." Although within a week after Pearl Harbor eleven thousand men enlisted in the navy and thousands more in the army, it was the draft that fueled the massive military buildup needed to win the war.

The call to arms reached into every corner of the nation, every segment of society. Farmboys from Iowa, streetwise youths from New York, and immigrants who struggled to speak English served with the four sons of President Roosevelt, actor Clark

Gable, and heavyweight boxing champion Joe Louis.

In just a few months military camps sprang up around the country and filled with millions of raw recruits. After only twenty-six weeks of basic training, newly minted soldiers or sailors were sent thousands of miles from home to fight, and die, for their country.

New Military Opportunities

The need for military personnel was so great that, for the first time, the armed forces allowed large numbers of women and blacks to enlist.

The Women's Army Corps (WAC), the navy's Women Accepted for Volunteer Emergency Service (WAVES), and the Women's Air Force Service Pilots (WASP) were created in 1942. Small numbers of women also served in the marines and Coast Guard. These women's auxiliary groups were separate from the male services. More than 100,000 women enlisted in 1942; another 200,000 would enlist before the end of the war.

Although women were not allowed to fight, many served in combat zones and some were killed, wounded, and captured. They worked as nurses, clerks, drivers, mechanics, pilots, and doctors, freeing men for combat. Women pilots, for example,

GO TO THE NEAREST RECRUITING STATION OF THE ARMED SERVICE OF YOUR CHOICE

Women were not allowed to fight in World War II, but women's auxiliaries to the regular military branches allowed women to fly airplanes, drive trucks, nurse the sick and wounded, and perform many other noncombat jobs. Women freed men for combat and also helped the war effort in many other ways.

were flight instructors and ferried airplanes from factories to military bases.

Unlike women, small numbers of blacks had always been allowed to serve in the armed forces; blacks have fought for their country in all of the nation's wars, including the Revolutionary War. In 1940s America, however, blacks faced discrimination

The Jewish Holocaust

The most barbaric and inhumane act in history was the cold-blooded extermination of approximately 6 million Jews by German soldiers and civilian officials during World War II. This genocide is known as the Holocaust.

Adolf Hitler appealed to the Germans' irrational and powerful feelings of anti-Semitism to win support for his National Socialist (Nazi) ideology. Hitler claimed Jews were responsible for Germany losing World War I, preached the supremacy of the Aryan race over Jewish people, and said Jews threatened German and Christian values.

When he became chancellor in 1933, Hitler enacted progressively harsher laws that took away rights from Jewish citizens and punished them for their alleged "crimes." Over the course of the war, Hitler put into action his so-called Final Solution to the Jewish problem. It was, simply, a decision to kill every Jew in Europe, the only systematic government effort in modern times to destroy an entire race.

Special units of the German army moved through Poland, slaying an estimated 2 million Jews in mass shootings. The units then rounded up Jews and used cattle cars to transport them to death camps at Auschwitz, Dachau, and Buchenwald in Germany and Chelmno, Majdeanek, and Treblinka in Poland.

As they arrived in these concentration camps, about a tenth of the Jews

Survivors of a Nazi concentration camp, appearing too weak to leave their bunk beds, stare numbly at the soldiers who freed them. The horror of what these survivors went through can be glimpsed in their faces.

were kept as slave labor. The men and women were systematically starved and worked to death. The rest were killed immediately in gas chambers disguised as showers..

Jews living in Germany, France, Holland, and other countries under German control were also rounded up and sent to their deaths.

But Jews were not the only prisoners and victims. Germans also rounded up and killed hundreds of thousands of people of Slavic and Gypsy descent, whom they also considered inferior to Aryans, as well as political dissidents. Only Jews, however, were marked for total annihilation.

in almost every aspect of life, including the armed forces; nevertheless, hundreds of thousands of blacks enlisted

in hopes of improving their lives.

In 1942, when heavyweight champion Joe Louis joined the army, he

Black soldiers train for a landing by sea near Norfolk, Virginia, in 1942.
Black soldiers, who encountered the same kind of racism in the military as
they had faced in civilian life, had to fight in segregated units during the war.

noted: "There may be a lot wrong in America, but there's nothing [Adolf] Hitler can fix."[18] By this Louis meant that though racism in America denied blacks many basic rights, they accepted the obligation to fight for their country against Germany and Japan. It was an attitude shared by the more than 1.5 million blacks who served in World War II.

As in civilian life, blacks were segregated. They served in separate units and, again as in civilian life, were usually assigned more menial jobs such as cooks, mess attendants, laborers, truck drivers, and cargo handlers. Black women who enlisted as nurses also had to serve in segregated units.

Many whites in the military felt blacks lacked the intelligence and fighting spirit needed for combat. This racist attitude continued during the war despite the heroism shown by blacks such as Dorie Miller at Pearl Harbor and the tens of thousands of black soldiers who were fighting.

The absurdity of racism was evident when black soldiers transported German prisoners of war through southern states by railroad. Because of southern segregation laws, black soldiers could not eat in the dining cars; their German prisoners could. The military even segregated storage of

U.S. infantrymen line up for "chow" while fighting in Belgium in January 1945. American soldiers in Europe had to cope with bitter winter weather as well as the physical and mental challenges of combat.

plasma, the liquid component of blood, so plasma from black donors would not be used in transfusions for whites. The irony is that the process for storing plasma was invented by Dr. Charles Richard Drew, a black man.

In mid-1940 only nine thousand blacks served in the army and a few thousand in the navy; the huge influx of black soldiers during the war multiplied not only their numbers but also tension between the races, and violent incidents occurred at some military bases between white and black soldiers. But overall, the war helped break down military racial barriers.

For the first time blacks were allowed to join the Marine Corps, pilot planes, and become officers. More than seven thousand blacks were promoted to the officer ranks during the war, laying the groundwork for an integrated military following World War II.

Fighting Around the World

Millions of young Americans who enlisted or were drafted soon found themselves scattered around the world. Places that they had known only as exotic names on world maps—Iwo Jima, Guadalcanal, Tarawa, Kasserine Pass, Sicily, Normandy, the Ardennes—became battlegrounds. Soldiers fought in the hot, humid jungles of the Pacific and the harsh, cold snows of France and Germany. But no matter where they fought, combat in World War II was a savage experience.

Bill Mauldin, the most famous cartoonist of the war, experienced the horror of war as an infantryman. Mauldin described the effect of combat on U.S. soldiers:

A soldier who has been a long time in the line does have a "look" in his eyes that anyone with practice can discern. It's a look of dullness, eyes that look without seeing, eyes that see without transferring any response to the mind. It's a look that is the display room for the thoughts that lie behind it— exhaustion, lack of sleep, tension for too long, weariness that is too great, fear beyond fear, misery to the point of numbness, a look of surpassing indifference to anything anybody can do to you. It's a look I dread to see of men. [19]

The War in the Pacific

The December 7 attack on Pearl Harbor signaled the start of a mighty Japanese offensive across the South Pacific. On December 8 Japan attacked U.S. forces on Wake Island, Guam, Midway Island, and Manila, the capital of the Philippine Islands. The Japanese also moved against the British possessions of Singapore and Hong Kong, Burma, and the Dutch East Indies.

The first few months of the war were bleak for America, which lost battle after battle to the Japanese. Tens of thousands of American soldiers were killed or captured. Even Gen. Douglas MacArthur, who commanded U.S. forces in the Philippines, was

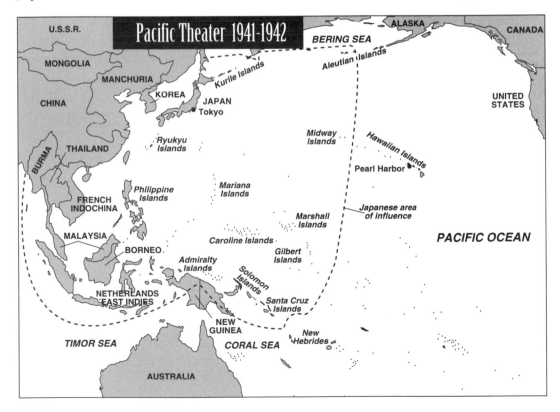

Ernie Pyle

Ernie Pyle, a small, timid-looking man who had always regretted being too young to fight in World War I, became the most popular journalist of World War II.

Pyle spent two and a half years on the front lines in Europe and the Pacific writing stories about average soldiers and the loneliness, fear, anger, sadness, and anguish they experienced in combat.

Pyle even won soldiers a pay raise with a column he wrote from Italy on March 1, 1944. Pyle argued that ground troops should receive the same extra hazard pay as fliers. The difference between combat and serving behind the lines, Pyle wrote, was that "one lives like a beast and dies in great numbers. The other is merely working away from home. . . . it seems to me the actual warrior deserves something to set him apart. And medals are not enough."

His influence was so great that by May Congress passed what was nicknamed the "Ernie Pyle Bill." Front-line soldiers received a 50 percent bonus in combat zones.

When the fighting was over in Europe, Pyle went to the Pacific. On April 18, 1945, he was killed by a sniper's bullet on a small island named Ie Shima. In his pocket was an unfinished column soberly describing the result of war:

Ernie Pyle's simple and moving stories about the experiences of American soldiers made him the nation's most beloved war correspondent. His newspaper stories about GIs helped people back home understand what the war was like for their loved ones.

"Dead men by mass production—in one country after another—month after month and year after year. Dead men in winter and dead men in summer. Dead men in such familiar promiscuity that they become monotonous. Dead men in such monstrous infinity that you come almost to hate them."

And Pyle had joined their ranks.

---

forced to retreat to Australia as the Japanese conquered all of the Philippines by May.

Fortunately for the navy, its aircraft carriers were at sea when Pearl Harbor was attacked. In the spring of 1942 they emerged as a key to victory, first in a daring raid on Japan and then in two pivotal sea battles.

On April 18 the aircraft carrier *Hornet* sailed to within 650 miles of Japan. Sixteen twin-engine B-25

An F6F takes off from the USS Yorktown *during the Battle of Midway. The U.S. victory in the sea battle was a turning point in the war because it stopped the Japanese advance in the South Pacific.*

bombers, each carrying two thousand pounds of bombs, took off to attack the cities of Tokyo, Nagoya, and Kobe in a raid led by Lt. Col. James Doolittle.

It was the first time the giant B-25s were successfully launched from a carrier. But because they were too big to land on the carriers after the attack, pilots were ordered to fly to China and land in friendly territory. Seventy

of the eighty-two crew members survived. Of the twelve that didn't make it, some crashed after running out of fuel or were shot down, captured, and executed by the Japanese.

Although the air attack was a huge morale boost for America, it caused little real damage in Japan. Within a few months, however, two naval battles helped turn the tide of war in the Pacific. U.S. intelligence, which had learned how to decode secret Japanese messages, discovered Japan would try to capture Port Moresby on New Guinea's south coast. This island base would enable the Japanese to invade Australia, their next objective.

Adm. Chester W. Nimitz ordered naval forces to the Coral Sea, where on May 3 they intercepted the Japanese invasion fleet. For several days the two sides fought a battle unique in history—the first naval engagement in which ships never fired a shot. All the fighting was done by planes launched from aircraft carriers. In fact, the ships never even came in sight of one another.

Japanese planes sank the carrier *Lexington*, a destroyer, and a tanker; American planes sank the carrier *Shoho* and a destroyer and damaged two other carriers. The United States came away with a narrow victory important for turning away the Japanese invasion. For the first time, Japan's offensive in the Pacific had been halted.

Japan next tried to capture Midway Island, a small atoll held by the United States about fifteen hundred miles west of Hawaii. Once again military intelligence learned of the attack and sent a large naval force to an area just north of Midway. The fleet included the carriers *Hornet*, *Enterprise*, and *Yorktown*. When the Japanese began their attack on June 4, U.S. forces caught them by surprise. In one day American planes destroyed nine Japanese ships, including four aircraft carriers, and crippled three battleships.

The Battle of Midway is considered the turning point in the war in the Pacific because the Japanese fleet was severely damaged and Japan suffered its first major defeat. For the rest of the war the Japanese were on the defensive as American military power continued to grow.

Now, it was time for the United States to attack Japan. On August 7 U.S. Marines landed on Guadalcanal, one of the southernmost of the Solomon Islands in the southwest Pacific. A fierce battle raged on Guadalcanal until February 1943, when the Japanese were finally driven from the island.

Although it would take two more years of bloody fighting and two atomic bombs to defeat the Japanese, the superiority of American military power had been established.

The War in Europe

When Germany invaded Poland in 1939 it had an unlikely ally—the Soviet Union. Although Adolf Hitler hated communism and the two countries had a history of mutual hostility, Hitler and Soviet leader Joseph Stalin negotiated a secret nonaggression pact on August 24. In exchange for its support, the Soviet Union was to receive half of Poland and take over the Baltic states of Latvia, Estonia, and Lithuania. Hitler received something more important—a free hand to invade the rest of Europe without having to fight a war on two fronts.

Although Great Britain and France declared war on Germany in September 1939, after Poland fell fighting ceased until April of 1940, when Germany invaded and quickly conquered Denmark and Norway. On May 10 Germany attacked Belgium and Holland as a prelude to invading France. Germany in 1914 had used a similar route through Belgium to attack France in World War I.

By mid-June Germany, with Italy as an ally, had conquered France, overwhelming French and English forces with a new form of warfare called *blitzkrieg*. German for "lightning war," the term referred to the speed with which Germany attacked. Hitler and his generals skillfully coordinated airplanes, tanks, and motorized infantry in massive offensives.

Hitler now unleashed his Luftwaffe

With St. Paul's Cathedral looming in the background, an aircraft spotter perches precariously on a roof in London. German planes relentlessly bombed London and other cities in the fall of 1940, but the Blitz was unable to break the spirit of the English.

(air force) on England. On July 10 German planes began bombing naval and air bases in England to soften the country up for an invasion. The air war became known as the Battle of Britain. In September Germany switched to bombing London and other cities to demoralize the civilian population. The young pilots of the British Royal Air Force took to the skies two and three times a day to defend their country against hundreds of German planes. It was a heroic fight; although crippled, Great Britain was able to withstand the aerial

Clark Gable

When Clark Gable flew combat missions during World War II, his greatest fear was that he would be shot down and captured. "If I ever fall into Hitler's hands, he will put me in a cage like a big gorilla. He'd exhibit me all over Germany," Gable said.

Hollywood's most popular actor would have been quite a catch for Adolf Hitler. In fact, when the Germans learned he was flying missions from a base in England, they offered a reward of $5,000, a promotion, and leave for any pilot who did shoot him down.

A superstar in movies like *Gone with the Wind*, Gable was forty-one when the war started and could easily have avoided service. But when his wife, actress Carole Lombard, died in a plane crash returning from a war bond rally in January 1942, Gable decided to enter the military.

He enlisted in the army and studied aerial gunnery and photography. The physical training was hard for Gable, who was much older than other recruits. So was the schooling. Never a good student, Gable resorted to memorizing facts as if they were lines in a movie script. He did this after everyone else went to sleep, while sitting on a toilet in the bathroom.

Assigned to produce a film about aerial gunnery, Gable went to an air base near London in 1943 and flew combat missions to take pictures and learn firsthand about the job.

Actor Clark Gable, dressed for a mission, chats with another flier at an airfield in England. Although his main assignment was to produce a movie on aerial gunnery, Gable also flew actual bombing missions and shot at enemy airplanes.

On Gable's first flight a 20-mm shell burst through the plane, tearing the heel off his boot and exiting just a couple of inches over his head. Gable several times manned a machine gun to fire at attacking German planes while on these missions.

Gable returned to Washington with thousands of feet of film he had risked his life for, only to find out his project had been superseded by another documentary dealing with the subject called *The Memphis Belle*. But Gable's footage was used in *Combat America*, *Wings Up*, and several other military training and promotional movies. He was discharged in June 1944.

assault, which eventually led Hitler to turn his attention from Britian to the Soviet Union as a target of conquest.

Germany in 1940 and early 1941 continued to consolidate its hold on western Europe. But in the spring of

1941 Hitler made his biggest mistake of the war. He decided to attack the Soviet Union over the protests of his generals, who had argued that fighting a two-front war could be disastrous. Hitler, convinced his armies were invincible, believed a German defeat of Russia would force Britian to surrender.

The German invasion began June 22 and at first had great success. By November German forces had pulled to within eighteen miles of the capital city of Moscow. Russia looked defeated. But the German offensive was stopped by the onset of the brutal Russian winter, the same elemental force that a century earlier had helped the Russians defeat an invasion by French emperor Napoléon Bonaparte.

Allied Turning Points

The U.S. entry into the fighting changed the course of the war in Europe. America began massive shipments of armaments to Britian and Russia, strengthening their exhausted forces, and Roosevelt promised soldiers as soon as they could be trained and equipped. The decision was made to engage Germany first because it was felt the navy could hold the Japanese in check in the Pacific.

The most pressing problem in early 1942 was the heavy loss of Allied ships to German submarines— called U-boats after the German word for submarine, *Unterseeboot*—and mines placed by the Germans in shipping lanes. During the first four months of 1942 U-boats sank eighty-two ships in the North Atlantic and almost two hundred in North American and Caribbean waters. U-boats ringed American ports. They operated so close to shore that sometimes civilians on land could see the attacks on merchant ships leaving U.S. ports.

The fight to ship matériel to the Allies in Europe has been called the

Gen. Dwight D. Eisenhower commanded American forces in Europe during World War II. His popularity as a war hero helped him win two terms as president in 1952 and 1956.

49

Battle of the Atlantic. The Allies established armed convoys to protect merchant ships. The convoys used sonar, a new technology that enabled the military to locate submarines and more often sink them. The Allies also devoted more than a thousand ships to sweeping for mines. By early 1943 Allied shipping losses had been greatly reduced, allowing needed supplies to flow freely.

While America was still building up its armed forces, Britian and Russia scored their first victories. In November 1942 the British defeated the Germans at El Alamein in North Africa. In January 1943 the Russians mounted a counteroffensive at Stalingrad that kept the Germans in retreat on the eastern front. The tide had turned.

American forces finally joined the fighting November 8, 1942, when they landed in Morocco and Algeria in North Africa. Gen. Dwight D. Eisenhower was commander of the invasion, which involved five hundred ships and 400,000 soldiers from the United States and Great Britain.

By May 1943 the Allies had driven the Germans out of North Africa and begun their assault on Europe. On July 10, 150,000 American and British forces landed in Sicily, an island off the coast of southern Italy. The suc-cessful invasion toppled the government of Fascist dictator Benito Mussolini, who had ruled Italy for two decades. Italy signed an armistice with the Allies in early August.

On September 2, U.S. forces landed in Salerno, Italy. German resistance was fierce and twelve thousand Americans were killed. The next few months saw the bloodiest fighting of the war between German and American forces. Allied control of Italy was not achieved until the following spring.

On June 6, 1944, D day, the Allies landed troops on France's Normandy coast in the largest single military operation in history. Eisenhower was again in charge of the invasion, known as Operation Overlord. Small landing craft ferried soldiers to shore, where they established footholds on heavily mined beaches under air attack and artillery and machine-gun fire. Americans landed at spots on the Normandy coast code-named Utah and Omaha while British and Canadian troops went ashore at nearby Gold, Juno, and Sword Beaches.

The sacrifice to win a narrow foothold on French soil was great: Americans suffered 4,649 casualties in just one day and combined the Allies suffered 10,000 casualties. But the Allies had finally breached Fortress

Europe; within a month a million sol-diers stormed ashore. With Germany besieged from the east by Russia, the Allies were now assured of victory.

By August the Allies liberated Paris. The following March American troops finally crossed the Rhine River into Germany. As Russian troops closed in on his underground bunker in Berlin, Hitler committed suicide on April 30. A day earlier, Mussolini had been executed by his own country-men. Germany surrendered on May 7.

The Death of FDR

By presidential proclamation May 8 was declared V-E Day—Victory in Europe Day. But the signature on the proclamation was that of Harry S Truman, not Franklin Delano Roosevelt. The man who was presi-dent longer than any other—twelve years, one month, and eight days—died April 12, 1945, at the presiden-tial retreat in Warm Springs, Georgia. He had won election to an unprece-dented fourth term just months before his death.

In the last year of the war FDR had been in failing health. Pictures from that period show a frail, weary chief executive who looked much older than his sixty-three years. Roosevelt died of circulatory and respiratory failure and other medical problems.

In May the nation, which had sadly mourned his passing a month earlier, joyously celebrated its victory over Germany. But the festivities were restrained. Americans knew they still had to defeat Japan.

The Atomic Bomb

The Allies had been steadily win-ning back territory in the South Pacific since early 1943, when they conquered Japanese forces at Guadalcanal. But the victories had come at a terrible human cost because the Japanese samurai (warrior) tradi-tion led soldiers to continue to fight ferociously and to the death, even when they were outnumbered and cut off from help. In the battle for the island of Okinawa, which ended June 21, 1945, after two and a half months of fighting, 13,000 Americans and more than 100,000 Japanese were killed. In battles toward the end of the war, many more Japanese were killed because of American superiority in weapons and supplies. Naval bombard-ments before island invasions killed tens of thousands of Japanese soldiers. Denied supplies because the Allies con-trolled the seas, Japanese soldiers were often near starvation and sometimes nearly out of ammunition. Thousands of Japanese soldiers also commited sui-cide rather than be captured.

The Birth of the Atomic Age

A letter in August 1939 to President Franklin D. Roosevelt from Albert Einstein and several other scientists was the catalyst for development of the atomic bomb.

They told Roosevelt that scientists would soon be able to split the atom, which would make possible "extremely powerful bombs of a new type." They also warned the president that Germany was trying to discover the secret to this terrible new weapon.

Einstein was a brilliant nuclear physicist who had fled Germany because of Jewish persecution. In the late '30s Einstein, Leo Szilard, Enrico Fermi, and other scientists investigated the secrets of the atom in laboratories at Columbia, Princeton, and the University of Chicago. The government at first took only a casual interest in this hypothetical weapon, but it did grant Fermi $6,000 to continue his work.

On December 2, 1942, Fermi achieved a chain reaction at the University of Chicago, splitting uranium atoms into a new form of matter called plutonium. He had found the key to unleashing the power of atomic energy, including the destructive potential of the atomic bomb.

The federal government then established the ultrasecret Manhattan Project, which brought together America's top scientists to perfect the atomic bomb. It was so secret that Vice President Truman did not learn about the bomb until more than a week after he became president.

On July 16, 1945, the work of tens of thousands of people and $2 billion in spending culminated in the first atomic bomb explosion in a desolate stretch of desert near Alamogordo, New Mexico. Within a month this new device had ended World War II and ushered in the atomic age.

Since their first victories in 1942, the Allies had worked their way north in the Pacific, capturing Tarawa, the Marianas, Saipan, the Philippines, Iwo Jima, and other territory as they advanced on Japan. In late 1944, from bases in China, the Allies began bombing runs that leveled areas of Japan and weakened its ability to fight back.

Although it would have taken many more months of bloody fighting, the outcome of the war was no longer in doubt in August 1945. And thanks to a terrifying new weapon, victory in the Pacific came just three months after V-E Day.

It started August 6, 1945, in the shape of a huge, billowing cloud of smoke and radioactive dust that rose, dark and ominous, from the atomic bomb the United States dropped on the Japanese city of Hiroshima.

"First there was a ball of fire changing in a few seconds to purple clouds and flames boiling and swirling upward," reported military

Only rubble remains after the atomic bomb blast that leveled Hiroshima and killed tens of thousands of people. Three days later the United States—the only country to ever use atomic weapons in time of war—dropped a second atomic bomb on Nagasaki.

observers flying in a second B-29 that accompanied the *Enola Gay,* which carried the bomb.

A flash was observed. . . . all agreed the light was intensely bright and the white cloud rose faster than the New Mexico [bomb] test, reaching thirty thousand feet in minutes. . . . It mushroomed at the top, broke away from the column and mushroomed again. The cloud was not turbulent. It went at least to forty thousand feet, flattening across its top at this level. [20]

The hellish scene at the base of the monstrous mushroom cloud was one of total devastation. The bomb struck with the force of 20,000 tons of TNT. It vaporized homes, flattened a 5-square-mile section of the city, and killed between 70,000 and 100,000 people.

When Japan still refused to surrender three days later, the United States dropped a second atomic bomb on Nagasaki, killing 40,000. Tens of thousands of people in the two cities would die later of radiation sickness.

Truman, only a few months after becoming president, had made the difficult decision to use the weapon. No one was really sure how great the devastation would be. But the test explosion of the first atomic bomb in history July 16 in Alamogordo, New Mexico, had proven the bomb's devastating capability.

A key factor in his decision, Truman said, was that he believed the bomb would save American and Japanese lives by shortening the war. It was estimated that both nations could have suffered as many as 1 million casualties had the conflict been brought to an end by conventional means. The massive firebomb raid on Tokyo on March 9–10, for example, had killed 80,000 people, destroyed more than 250,000 buildings, and gutted a quarter of the city.

In the weeks before the first atomic bomb was dropped, the United States had warned Japan to surrender or suffer the consequences of a powerful new weapon. But military and political leaders had refused. Once they realized the cataclysmic power of the atomic bomb, however, they had no other choice. Japan surrendered August 14.

The Price of Victory

Even though the atomic bomb shortened the war, America paid a terrible price for victory. During the war, silken banners decorated with blue stars hung from the windows of countless homes. Each blue star represented a son or daughter who was in the service. When their loved ones died, families sadly replaced blue stars with gold stars.

In World War II, 292,131 U.S. soldiers were killed in combat, 675,000 were wounded, and 139,709 became prisoners of war or were listed as missing in action (MIA). Many MIAs were never found and could only be presumed dead, and many prisoners died in captivity. Tens of thousands were disabled by war injuries and an estimated 6,000 American civilians died, almost all overseas.

The Sullivan family of Waterloo, Iowa, has been singled out for the loss it suffered. After a childhood friend was killed at Pearl Harbor five Sullivan brothers—Joseph, Francis, Albert, Madison, and George—enlisted together in the navy. All five died November 14, 1942, when the USS *Juneau* was sunk in the Pacific. The tragedy led to a ruling that family members were prohibited from serving on the same ship.

Victory never comes cheaply in war.

Chapter Four

Actor Macdonald Carey (center) shakes hands with Brian Donlevy as Carey prepares for an aerial mission during Wake Island. *This film about the actual battle for Wake Island helped stir the pride of Americans.*

The Movies Go to War

"We'll blacken your skies and burn your cities to the ground and make you get down on your knees and beg for mercy. This is your war. . . . You wanted it. . . . You started it. And now you're going to get it, and it won't be finished until your dirty little empire is wiped off the face of the earth." [21] When actor Dana Andrews delivered that speech in 1944 in *The Purple Heart*, people in

theaters across America stood up and cheered. They whistled, applauded, and stamped their feet at the bravery and defiance the popular star's character showed to his Japanese captors.

The movie tells the story of the air raid on Tokyo in April 1942, in which U.S. pilots attacked Japan from an aircraft carrier. In the movie, the Japanese grill the crew of one of the planes they shoot down to find out if

55

This courtroom scene is from The Purple Heart, *a film about U.S. fliers who were shot down after bombing Japan. Standing in front of the captive Americans is the sadistic Japanese officer who tortured them but failed to make them reveal military secrets.*

their captives took off from a ship or from an air base in China. The Japanese fear that the United States has a land base that will allow planes to bomb Japan repeatedly.

In the course of a mock civil trial, crew members are brutally tortured but refuse to talk. Finally, they have to make a choice—each is urged to secretly reveal where their planes came from; if no one does, the Japanese will execute them. When the airmen remain united in silence, Dana Andrews gives his stirring speech. The movie ends with the soldiers being led away to their deaths. The brutal Japanese general who failed to make them talk commits suicide.

Audiences left the theater feeling reassured; the film showed that Americans were braver than and morally superior to the Japanese. *The Purple Heart* and other war films lifted the spirits of civilian and military audiences alike, pumping up their patriotism and making them feel they were sacrificing sons, husbands, and themselves for a noble cause.

Office of War Information director Elmer Davis once said, "The easiest way to inject a propaganda idea into most people's minds is to let it go in through the medium of an entertainment picture, when they do not realize that they're being propagandized." [22]

During World War II, the use of propaganda films was considered just another way to wage war. The Axis powers were also making movies that glorified their countries and justified their own reasons for going to war. Hollywood fought back cinematically between 1942 and 1945 with about 375 movies that were clearly propagandistic.

Movies that came out in the first months of the war served as effective propaganda simply by helping unite the nation. *A Yank on the Burma Road*, *Wake Island*, *Bataan*, and other films stirred patriotic feelings and made people feel the nation was right in going to war. Other major themes were the need for everyone to make sacrifices to win the war, the superiority of America's democratic way of life to fascism, and the certainty of victory once the United States was committed to the war.

The Dream Factory

Known as "the dream factory," Hollywood was dominated by major studios such as MGM (Metro-Goldwyn-Mayer), 20th Century-Fox, Warner Brothers, and Paramount. When America went to war, Hollywood quickly geared up to bring the drama of that conflict to the silver screen. In the first six months of the war, studios cranked out more than seventy war-related films.

Films distributed right after Pearl Harbor had a huge impact on a nation still horrified and disheartened by the sneak attack. Movies like *Wake Island* told the story of the valiant defense of the small South Pacific island by U.S. Marines. A *New York Times* review called it "a film which should surely bring a surge of pride to every patriot's breast." [23] Paramount was in such a rush to make the movie that it had to hold up final production for two weeks until the real battle of Wake Island was finally over.

Because the war was a vital part of everyone's daily life, studios injected the war theme into many different types of movies. Screen characters such as Sherlock Holmes, Charlie Chan, and the Dead End Kids—a group of happy-go-lucky youths one step away from being juvenile delinquents—all won battles against German and Japanese foes.

Even Johnny Weissmuller, the most famous screen Tarzan, fights the

The Studio System

The motion picture industry in the '40s was dominated by the so-called studio system. Five major and three minor studios had virtual control over what movies were made, who would star in them, and which theaters could show them.

The major studios were Paramount, MGM (Metro-Goldwyn-Mayer), 20th Century-Fox, Warner Brothers, and RKO (Radio-Keith-Orpheum). Universal, Columbia, and United Artists were smaller studios.

Actors and actresses, directors, writers, and other production workers were all under contract to work only for one studio. Actors and actresses received a weekly salary and had to act in any film in which they were cast.

A large part of the power of the major studios stemmed from the fact that they owned chains of theaters in which they usually showed their own pictures. Although major studios owned only three thousand of eighteen thousand theaters in the nation, in 1945 those theaters generated more than 70 percent of all box office receipts.

The studio system began to fail at the end of the decade because of the rise of independent studios, the challenge from television, and a U.S. Supreme Court ruling that found studios guilty of antitrust activities, essentially illegal business practices. The court ordered studios to sell their theater chains, which greatly weakened the power they had over the movie industry.

Nazis in *Tarzan Triumphs* (1943) when German soldiers parachute into his jungle home to gain control of oil and tin reserves. The Ape Man ignores the Germans at first but audiences cheered when Weissmuller finally declares, "Tarzan make war on Nazis." With jungle animals as his allies, Tarzan easily defeats the Germans.

The Golden Age of Film

But studios in this golden age of films made movies that dealt with other subjects as well. In westerns, the legendary John Wayne and Randolph Scott competed for fans with singing cowboys Roy Rogers and Gene Autry. Mysteries like *Double Indemnity* (1944) with Edward G. Robinson and *The Maltese Falcon* (1941), starring Humphrey Bogart as the hard-boiled detective Sam Spade, intrigued fans throughout the decade.

Comedies also helped people forget their worries in a time of anxiety and stress. Bud Abbott and Lou Costello, who starred in fifteen films between 1941 and 1945, including *In the Navy* and *Buck Privates*, were two of the decade's biggest stars. Bob Hope, Bing Crosby, and Dorothy Lamour appeared in a string of box office hits like *The Road to Singapore* and *The Road to Morocco*. Movie shorts with the Three Stooges, who appeared in 190 such films between 1934 and 1959, and other comedy greats were huge hits.

Lighthearted musicals such as *Meet Me in St. Louis* (1944) and *State Fair* (1945) also became a staple of the decade. One of the biggest war hits was the musical *Yankee Doodle Dandy*, starring James Cagney. The movie tells the story of George M. Cohan, whose popular songs, including "Yankee Doodle Dandy" and "Over There," helped inspire the nation during World War I. The movie stirred patriotic feelings and reminded Americans that they had beaten Germany in an earlier war.

The Bureau of Motion Pictures

The federal government was fully aware of the tremendous impact movies had on the public. Once the war began, it moved quickly to harness that power. To ensure that movies were patriotic and fully supported the war, in April 1942 the government created the Bureau of Motion Pictures (BMP), part of the Domestic Branch of the Office of War Information (OWI), the government propaganda agency.

OWI issued and constantly updated the "Government Information Manual for the Motion Picture

James Cagney, front and center in this scene from Yankee Doodle Dandy, *usually played movie tough guys. But in this patriotic musical songfest, he starred as George M. Cohan, who wrote popular World War I songs such as "Over There."*

Newsreels

For several decades, newsreels had enabled viewers to watch and learn about historic events taking place around the world. They became even more popular during World War II, with some theaters showing nothing but newsreels to satisfy the public's appetite for war footage.

The films were popular because they helped moviegoers feel closer to sons, daughters, husbands, and fathers serving far from home in the armed forces. And because the newsreels always had a positive tone about the U.S. war effort, they made people feel more hopeful the United States would prevail in the fighting.

Newsreels were able to transport moviegoers to the fighting in Europe or the Pacific. Footage of aerial combat, invasions of islands in the South Pacific, and other combat thrilled audiences in a way that newspaper and radio stories could not.

The newsreels also showed how civilians were doing their part for the war effort by collecting scrap, buying war bonds, and dealing with rationing. They helped the nation feel a sense of unity during one of the most traumatic periods in its history.

Newsreels remained a key way for people to learn about their world through the end of the decade, before television newscasts made them obsolete. Television was able to show the same type of news from around the world, and it did it on a nightly basis right in the living rooms of every family.

Industry," which told studios how their movies could help the war effort. It also explained why America was fighting and outlined the philosophy underlying the nation's democratic way of life. The manual specifically asked studio executives to consider seven questions when planning a movie. They included "Will this picture help win the war?" and "If it is an 'escape' picture, will it harm the war effort by creating a false picture of America, her Allies, or the world we live in?" [24]

OWI was also concerned about the message movies would deliver to foreign audiences. It feared movies would indicate Americans had loose morals or were not dedicated to winning the war.

The OWI had no real censorship powers over the film industry, however, and had to rely on studios' voluntary compliance. OWI reviewed more than sixteen hundred scripts during the war. Any themes, situations, or characters OWI considered negative to the war effort were returned with a request for script changes; sometimes OWI even rewrote dialogue.

Studios complied when, for example, OWI asked them not to

portray the plight of U.S. prisoners of war in Japanese camps. The agency felt such films might cause the Japanese to retaliate by hurting POWs. Hollywood went along with the ban until 1943, when the government issued public reports on the subject. That cleared the way for films like *The Purple Heart*, which reveled in revealing Japanese brutality toward American prisoners.

Studios also met OWI requests for movies on particular war issues. Examples included films that stressed the heroism and sacrifices made by the Soviet Union and China. Nelson Poynter, a newspaper publisher who headed the bureau's Hollywood office, bluntly asked studios to "Give us a Mrs. Miniver of China or Russia." [25] *Mrs. Miniver*, which in 1942 won Academy Awards for best picture and best actress for Greer Garson, showcased the bravery of the English during the Blitz.

Another example of a film made at OWI's request was 1943's *Action in the North Atlantic*, starring Humphrey Bogart and Raymond Massey. The Warner Brothers film highlighted the bravery of the merchant marine in transporting supplies across the Atlantic Ocean to the Allies. The movie starts and ends with messages from President Roosevelt on the importance of civilian sailors to the war effort. *Action in the North Atlantic* also deals with several other issues OWI wished to publicize.

In one scene in a bar, a loud-mouthed sailor named Gus describes a convoy he has just seen leaving port. One of the government's wartime concerns was that "loose lips sink ships," a warning never to talk about military activity. Bogart, as First Mate Joe Rossi, tells Gus to shut up; when he keeps talking, Bogart patriotically knocks him out.

In another scene a sailor criticizes a fellow merchant marine for not signing up for another supply run. A third intervenes, saying that though the sailor is wrong he can do whatever he wants. He says that's what the war is all about—guaranteeing people freedom of choice. Other sailors then lecture the holdout about the importance of their job and the need to win the war. In the end, of course, he signs up again.

OWI used *Pittsburgh*, a 1942 Universal film about the steel industry starring John Wayne, Randolph Scott, and Marlene Dietrich, to boost defense industries. Near the end of the film the plant receives a government award for steel production. Scott then delivers an impassioned speech about winning the war that is taken almost

In this scene from the sentimental Since You Went Away, *Claudette Colbert reads a letter to her daughters. Kneeling is Shirley Temple, the famous child star.*

word for word from OWI material. The speech is heavy-handed; even Lowell Mellett, head of the Bureau of Motion Pictures, said critically, "The propaganda sticks out disturbingly." [26]

Since You Went Away (1944), with Claudette Colbert and Shirley Temple, was one of many movies that focused on life at home. It highlighted such key OWI messages as the importance of the sacrifices families made while loved ones were fighting in the war. In this case, the family, although finan-

cially well off, even rents a spare room in their home. OWI saw this as an important message in a time when there was a severe housing shortage.

Propaganda themes often developed into movie stereotypes. The bureau recommended multiethnic military units to show that diversity was one of America's greatest strengths. In *The Purple Heart*, the last names of crew members include Ross (Anglo-Saxon), Greenbaum (Jewish), Canelli (Italian), and Skvoznick (Slavic). This multiethnic mix was a staple of nearly every war movie. The bureau hoped to counter propaganda from Germany and Japan, both of which claimed that America's "melting pot" society made it a "mongrel" nation whose people did not have the courage or the will to win a war.

Movies also stereotyped the enemy. German soldiers were dangerous and sometimes cruel, but they weren't monsters. Only members of the Nazi Party were characterized as truly evil, and many movies portrayed "good Germans" who helped fight the Nazis. But Japanese soldiers were always cruel, treacherous, and sneaky, subhumans who were inherently inferior to whites.

Actor Lloyd Nolan comments in *Guadalcanal Diary*, for example, "Well, it's kill or be killed—because they ain't people." [27] In *Objective Burma*, after seeing bodies of soldiers mutilated by the Japanese, Henry Hull screams, "They're degenerate, moral idiots. Stinking little savages. Wipe them out, I say, wipe them off the face of the earth." [28] It was a stereotype that was tinged with the kind of "yellow peril" racism against Asians that had been evident at other times in U.S. history.

One irony is that Chinese American actors, whose own homeland was under attack by Japan, played all the Japanese roles. Because of anti-Japanese feelings during the war, Japanese Americans were not allowed to act in films.

African Americans, however, were often left out of this ethnic mix. In movies, blacks were usually portrayed as slow-witted, comical characters, usually maids or servants. *Bataan* (1943) was one of the few films in which a black actor, Kenneth Spencer, played a hero. The film was based on the actual battle and Spencer's character fought and died alongside such stars as Robert Taylor, Thomas Mitchell, and Lloyd Nolan. Producer Dore Schary of MGM included a black in the multicultural mix even though it proved unpopular with some Americans, who resented a black being cast as a hero: "I put one [black] in *Bataan*, just put one in, that's all.

Katharine Hepburn and Turhan Bey in Dragon Seed, *a movie about Chinese resistance to the Japanese during World War II. Although the two actors appear a bit silly in the makeup that unsuccessfully tried to make them look Chinese, the film was a hit in the United States.*

We got a lot of letters from people complaining." [29]

More Foreign Policy

The government used Hollywood to polish the image of two of its wartime allies. Studios responded with films like *Dragon Seed* (1944), in which brave Chinese peasants risk their lives to fight the Japanese occupation. The American public loved it even though Walter Huston, Katharine Hepburn, and other Caucasian stars didn't make very convincing Chinese peasants.

Casablanca

Casablanca, winner of the Academy Award for best picture of 1942, is one of the classic films of the 1940s. Starring Humphrey Bogart and Ingrid Bergman, two of the era's greatest stars, *Casablanca* was released in November 1942 during the Allied invasion of North Africa. Warner Brothers even moved up its release date by two months when the invasion was made public.

Bogart plays Rick Blaine, a cynical American who owns the Café Americäin, a nightclub in the North African city occupied by the Germans. Bergman is Ilsa, his former lover, who is fleeing the Nazis with her husband, a French resistance leader, and secret documents that will help the Allies in the war against Germany.

Rick and Ilsa had met in wartorn Paris and fallen in love at a time when she thought her husband had been killed by the Germans. When Ilsa learns he is alive she leaves Rick without explaining why. They still love each other when they meet again in Casablanca.

Rick has an exit visa that could provide the couple safe passage, but he needs it himself to flee Casablanca. The film is set in the days just before Pearl Harbor is attacked. When *Casablanca* was released, Rick's indecision over whether to help the couple was compared to America's indecision over fighting Germany and Japan.

In one of the most dramatic of all movie endings, Rick shoots a German officer so Ilsa and her husband can escape on a waiting plane. Before Ilsa leaves he tells her, "I'm no good at being noble, but it doesn't take much to see that the problems of three little people don't count for a hill of beans in this crazy world."

Rick has finally realized that opposing the Germans, at any cost, is more important than personal happiness.

Russia, especially, needed a new image because it had been considered a foe of the United States since the Communist takeover of 1917. *Mission to Moscow* and *The North Star*, both made in 1943, were two movies that portrayed Russians as heroic fighters. The film trade newspaper *Variety* claimed, "War has put Hollywood's traditional concept of the Muscovites through the wringer, and they have come out shaved, washed, sober, [and] good to their families." [30]

The War Department

The War Department's Bureau of Public Relations also reviewed films that featured the army, navy, or army air corps. This agency did have some power over the studios because it provided studios with technical advisers, access to military bases, and even soldiers as extras to help make films. If the War Department didn't like a film, it could refuse to cooperate, and the department's help was vital to a film's realism and to holding down costs.

Sometimes, OWI and the War Department disagreed over a film's content. In early 1943 OWI objected to several elements in the Warner Brothers' film *Air Force*. The agency objected to a plot that hinged on disloyalty by Japanese American citizens. But because the War Department liked the film, even lending the studio a Flying Fortress bomber to make the movie, Warner Brothers felt secure in ignoring OWI's objections.

More than Entertainment

The film industry's contribution to the war effort was much greater than making popular films. Studios helped produce training films for the military and for defense industries, documentaries, and government-sponsored films.

The government, with Hollywood's help, released many short educational movies on wartime issues ranging from how to grow a victory garden to the importance of women in the defense industry. The films were all guaranteed an outlet because some twelve thousand movie theaters promised to show any picture that had the approval of the War Activities Committees, a group of motion picture industry leaders. Even Disney Studios, which in the 1940s created

animated classics like *Pinocchio*, *Dumbo*, and *Bambi*, made movies for the war effort. Disney produced *Victory Through Air Power*, a documentary that described the role of the army air corps, and Donald Duck appeared in patriotic short films urging people to collect scrap metal and pay their income taxes.

The government created military units composed entirely of actors, directors, writers, and other movie personnel. These special units made training films and documentaries and shot historical war footage. The army signal corps created the *Why We Fight* series of films, which explained the causes and progress of the war, why the United States was fighting, and what it hoped to achieve. *Why We Fight* was directed by Frank Capra, a lieutenant colonel in the signal corps and one of the greatest directors of his era. His movie credits include such classics as *Mr. Smith Goes to Washington* and the sentimental *It's A Wonderful Life* (1946).

The first part of the *Why We Fight* series won the Academy Award for best documentary of 1942. The series as a whole is considered by many to be the most powerful American propaganda ever produced. Capra used historical footage, film reenactments, charts, maps, and other devices to explain the ideological and historical

Donald Duck

One of the most unlikely draftees of World War II was a little guy with flat feet, a speech impediment, a crabby personality—and feathers!

The draft notice for Donald Fauntleroy Duck (who would have guessed *that* was his middle name) arrived March 24, 1942. In his first war cartoon he was inducted and experienced all the miserable experiences of human recruits. Donald became a one-duck army and even took on Adolf Hitler in 1943 in *Der Fuehrer's Face*, subtitled *Donald Duck in Nutzi Land.*

Der Fuehrer's Face, which won an Academy Award for best short feature, was pure anti-Nazi propaganda. In the cartoon the popular Disney character dreams he is living in Germany. Poor Donald is bullied around by Nazis and, in one sequence, sees Hitler's face wherever he turns. His misadventures, though comical, were meant to highlight the horror of Nazi rule. When Donald finally wakes up, he is wearing pajamas that look like the American flag and he exclaims how much he loves the United States.

Donald Duck was the war's biggest animated star. He fought the Axis powers

Donald Duck happily hugs a miniature Statue of Liberty after waking up from his nightmare in Der Fuehrer's Face. He was a real hero during the war by appearing in cartoons that had a variety of patriotic messages.

in cartoons and starred in government films, including *The Spirit of '43*, which stressed that paying taxes was patriotic.

The plucky duck was a favorite of soldiers and appeared on more than four hundred military insignia that Disney Studios designed. His face and figure were also painted on airplanes, submarines, bombs, and torpedoes as soldiers lovingly adopted him as a mascot and good luck charm.

reasons underlying the war. By making Americans aware of why the nation needed to fight Germany and Japan, the films helped unite the nation.

Movie studios also helped the war effort by providing free prints of forty-three thousand movies to soldiers overseas, boosting the morale of mil-

lions of soldiers hungry for a taste of home. Maj. Gen. Charles H. Bonesteel once said "motion pictures are as necessary to the men as rations." [31]

A Universal Commitment

The need for universal commitment to the war effort was perhaps the most important wartime message. It even became part of a low–budget picture called *Seven Miles from Alcatraz*, a movie about convicts who escape from the island prison but risk recapture to fight a band of Nazi spies. Says one escapee, "We may be rats, crooks, and murderers—but we're Americans!"[32]

B Movies and Serials

Moviegoers in the 1940s got a lot for their dime or quarter (the price of admission went up on weekends). In addition to a feature film, the show could include a newsreel, one or more cartoons, and an episode of the latest adventure serial.

Theaters often showed double features: this two-films-for-the-price-of-one concept began in the '30s to boost attendance during the Great Depression.

The second film would be a "B movie," shorter and more cheaply made. B movies were westerns, horror or science fiction films, musicals, and comedies that generally featured unknown actors. However, stars like John Wayne, Robert Taylor, and Joan Crawford began their careers in B movies.

Another movie bargain was the serial. Each serial had twelve to fifteen episodes that were about twenty minutes long and shown in weekly installments. Each episode had a "cliffhanger" ending to hook audiences into coming back the following week.

Serials, which started in the 1930s but were still very popular in the 1940s, featured masked villains, chaotic violence, and fantastic characters. Batman, Superman, the Green Hornet, Dick Tracy, and the Shadow all starred in serials, which were cheaply made but fun to watch.

These youngsters eagerly wait to see films with Charlie Chan, the Chinese detective, and Joe Palooka, the heavyweight champion from the newspaper comic section. Their cowboy apparel probably means they will also be treated to the latest installment in a cowboy serial.

Buster Crabbe, who played the comic strip character Flash Gordon in several very popular serials, was the most famous actor in this type of film. Women also starred in serials, with several "jungle queen" heroines featured in serials like *Panther Girl of the Kongo*, *The Tiger Woman*, and *Jungle Girl*.

Chapter Five

The excitement of this little girl can be matched only by her father's delight as he is finally able to hug his daughter at the end of World War II. Touching reunions like this were the most important victories produced by the end of the fighting.

Postwar Life

The victory over Japan unleashed a giant celebration that engulfed the nation. The war that had consumed the lives of Americans for nearly four years was finally over. But when the nation was done congratulating itself, the challenge of converting to a peacetime economy remained. This included putting to work almost 12 million men and women who were released from the armed forces.

After World War I the nation had experienced an economic recession as it switched from making weapons to producing consumer goods. After the dark days of the Great Depression, the thought of unemployment and more economic hardship was frightening.

But the postwar transition was fairly smooth and the now roaring economy barely skipped a beat. As soon as Japan surrendered, the federal government allowed factories and businesses to return to general consumer production. The government gradually ended rationing, although sugar was still so scarce it was rationed through June 1948.

Government economic planners had estimated reconversion could swell the ranks of the unemployed to as many as 10 million. Although reconversion was not entirely painless, unemployment never reached such heights. In the first year after the war unemployment never rose higher than 3 million. Because new enterprises were starting up daily, people displaced by the changeovers quickly found work again in what was now the world's strongest, richest economy.

One factor that made a successful changeover possible was that by the end of the war, Americans had amassed nearly $140 billion in savings. They used their nest eggs to satisfy a pent-up hunger for new cars, tires, refrigerators, homes, and other products the war had denied them. Plenty of capital allowed industries to retool to make those products and businesses rushed to make the switch, knowing they would be successful.

Within a few months automakers in Detroit quit making tanks and planes and started turning out new cars again. People rushed to buy the cars, creating long lines in showrooms as they viewed the first new models since 1941. The same enthusiasm infected other industries.

A second major reason the conversion went smoothly was that the war had destroyed the industrial infrastructure of many nations. Factories, electric power plants, homes, buildings, and businesses in England, Germany, Japan, France, Italy, and other countries were reduced to rubble or heavily damaged. These nations now turned to the United States, which had been untouched by the war, for consumer products and food.

It took years and even decades for some countries to rebuild their shattered economies. Meanwhile, the U.S. economy soared for two decades as it filled the global industrial and manufacturing void the war had created.

Returning GIs

When the United States defeated Germany, American families started demanding the return of their loved ones as quickly as possible. Within months, millions of soldiers and sailors began coming home from Europe on packed troopships. In December 1945 alone 1.5 million service personnel returned. The demobilization speeded up after Japan surrendered and contin-

World War II Casualties

Estimates of total World War II casualties range up to 45 to 50 million people, more than any war in history. That figure includes civilians who died during battles, from disease caused by the war, and of starvation.

The Soviet Union death toll was by far the highest—18 million, including 7 million civilians. Germany had 3.5 million combat deaths and nearly 800,000 civilian deaths, Japan 1.3 million combat deaths and more than 670,000 civilian deaths, and China 1.3 million combat deaths. There is no reliable estimate on the number of Chinese civilians killed, but estimates reach the tens of millions.

Poland suffered only 122,178 combat fatalities but the second-highest total of civilian deaths, 5.6 million. More than half the 5.7 million Jews killed in the Holocaust were Polish.

The fighting that raged in Europe and Asia for more than a decade consumed the lives of most of an entire generation of young men from many countries. Entire countries, such as Japan and Germany, were left in near total ruin and

A private receives blood plasma after being wounded while fighting in Sicily in 1943. World War II took tens of millions of lives, killing not only soldiers but also innocent civilians.

other nations were damaged so heavily that it took many years to rebuild and return to a semblance of normal life.

The war's destruction was one of the reasons the United States, untouched by the carnage, emerged so strong from the conflict.

ued until the armed forces had been reduced to about 1 million.

Returning GIs faced a triple adjustment. They had to become part of their families again, they had to find work, and they had to readjust to civilian life. For the most part they enjoyed a successful homecoming. A grateful government made the task easier by promising military personnel $20 a week for 52 weeks after they were discharged. The funds helped members of the "52-20 Club," as servicemen were called, to find new jobs and make the transition back to civilian life.

The Servicemen's Readjustment Act of 1944, more commonly called the GI Bill of Rights, also helped soldiers reestablish their private lives. It guaranteed them loans to buy homes or start businesses and helped millions of GIs get a college education by paying up to $500 a year toward tuition and books, at the time a sum large enough to pay for an education at most colleges and universities. Veterans also received a personal living expense of $65 a month if they were single and $90 if they were married so they would not have to work while they went to school.

The GI Bill enabled nearly 8 million people to attend college or trade school or receive some other form of advanced training. Singer Tony Bennett, for example, studied voice under the GI Bill before beginning his long, successful career as one of America's favorite crooners.

This young soldier arriving home receives a warm family welcome from loved ones, who may not have seen him for years. He surely brought home his own hope for a bright future, one that would never again include going off to war.

Family Life

The homecomings were joyous. The sons, daughters, and spouses who had been gone for so long were finally back. But once the tearful homecomings were over, some veterans had a difficult time readjusting to family life. They had to become reacquainted with their children and their spouses after long absences. In some cases, fathers were seeing sons and daughters for the first time. Children had to get used to having a father around the house again.

Many young couples who had married in haste during the war had marital problems. After years of separation, some of them felt like they were married to strangers. Women had enjoyed new freedom and responsibility during the war and many had worked for the first time. Some women now had a difficult time readjusting to having their husbands make all the decisions. Marital problems for returning servicemen led to a record national divorce rate in 1946 of 4.6 divorces per thousand—more than twice the 2.0 rate in 1940.

New mass production techniques that held down the cost of homes and sped-up construction gave rise after World War II to suburban living. Tens of thousands of homes sprang up after the war in housing tracts called Levittowns, a name from the first such housing project in Long Island, New York.

Family life was also affected by the fact that many women wanted to continue working. During the war more women than ever before held jobs, making up 35 percent of the workforce in 1945. Although the percentage of women dropped to 29.6 percent in 1946, that was still more than 5 percent higher than 1940 and it continued to rise throughout the rest of the decade.

The postwar years saw a huge increase in the number of new families as returning GIs married and the new couples began having children. The birth rate jumped from 19.9 per thousand in 1944 to 25.8 per thousand in 1947. It remained high for more than a decade in a period that was called the "baby boom." Children born in this era became known as "baby boomers."

The Birth of the Suburbs

One of the biggest postwar problems Americans had to cope with was a severe lack of housing. Shortly after the war ended, a Senate committee estimated the nation needed 5 million new housing units. The committee's report described young couples across the country who were forced to move in with their parents or set up housekeeping in "garages, coal sheds, chicken coops, barns, tool sheds, granaries and smokehouses." [33] The shortage was caused by a lack of new home construction during the Great Depression and the war, the migration by millions of people to new areas of the country during the war, and the postwar flood of marriages and births.

One solution to the shortage changed American life forever—the birth of the suburbs. In 1947 William Levitt started mass-producing small, affordable homes on a former potato field on Long Island, New York. The prefab, Cape Cod–style houses sold for $6,990, which made them affordable to average people. Levitt also decided that the nation's first mass-produced housing project, which became known as Levittown, would be open only to returning veterans and their families.

Until the postwar era, suburban areas outside of major cities had mainly been inhabited by the rich. But Levitt's idea quickly caught on and new suburbs sprang up around the nation. New techniques in construction that had been developed during the war made homes more affordable and drastically cut building time. In only four years Levitt was able to put up 17,447 homes on Long Island.

This new type of housing made it possible for more people than ever before to realize the American dream of home ownership. In fact, ownership of single-family homes grew more in the decade following the war than it had in the previous 150 years.

Organized Labor

One of the reasons Americans were able to buy more homes and consumer products than ever before was that labor unions had become stronger, winning higher wages and greater benefits for workers. Although there were some labor problems during the war, less than 1 percent of production time was lost to strikes or walkouts.

By 1945 unions, which had battled for survival in the '20s and '30s, had tripled their prewar membership to 15 million. With the war over, unions quickly began flexing their muscle. In November 1945, 180,000 United Auto Workers walked off the assembly line at General Motors. It was the first of a wave of postwar strikes that hit steel mills, railroads, coal mines, and other major industries and put millions of workers on the picket lines.

The reason for the labor unrest was that workers believed they deserved a bigger share of the profits big companies were making. Although

This scene of labor protest in San Francisco was one that was repeated end-lessly across the nation after the war. Labor unrest swept the country as work-ers demanded higher wages and management fought to reduce the power and gains unions had won during the last decade.

wages and benefits had improved during the war years, profits had far outpaced these increases.

President Truman responded in early 1946 by creating a fact-finding panel to investigate wages. At the time the average hourly wage at General Motors was $1.10; workers wanted $1.45 and the company offered $1.20. The government report, taking into account a 30 percent increase in the cost of living from prewar levels, recommended a raise of 19.5 cents for autoworkers and 18.5 cents for steelworkers. Both unions eventually set-

tled on 18.5-cent increases, which became a national standard and helped end other strikes.

Republicans campaigned against the increasing power of labor unions in 1946, when 4.6 million workers staged strikes in various industries. When Republicans won control of both the House and Senate for the first time in years, they struck back at labor. In 1947 Congress passed the Taft-Hartley Act, which limited the power of unions. The bill imposed a sixty-day "cooling off" period before a strike or lockout could be called, barred strikes that would endanger national health and safety, and imposed several other restrictions on unions.

Taft-Hartley weakened labor, but not seriously. Unions continued to fight for a bigger slice of the economic pie throughout the rest of the decade, and they went on strike when they felt it necessary.

Black Americans

During the war black Americans had shared in the sacrifices that all Americans made to achieve victory. They had suffered the loss of sons and daughters in combat, endured rationing and other restrictions, and worked long hours in defense plants to produce the weapons that secured the victory. What they had achieved gave many blacks a new sense of pride in themselves that spilled over into the rest of the decade.

In 1945 a black newspaper columnist wrote, "I do not believe that Negroes will stand idly by and see these newly opened doors of economic opportunity closed in their faces. Nor will Negro GIs permit our propaganda machine to forget that it did the world's best job when it sought to convince these same Negroes that this was really a war for democracy and against fascism." [34]

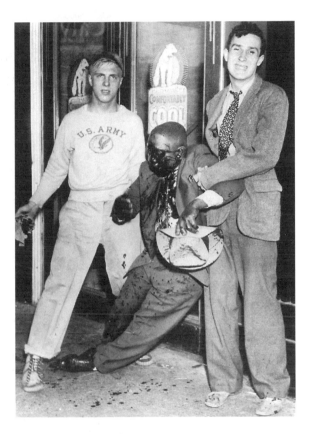

Two young men help a black man who was beaten during the 1943 race riot in Detroit. The mass migration of blacks to northern cities during the war created new racial tensions in many parts of the country.

The war had opened up new opportunities for black men and women in the military and in the private sector. It also created a mass migration of some 700,000 blacks from the south to urban cities in the north and California, forever changing the nation's demographics. During the

Jackie Robinson

Jackie Robinson is best known for breaking baseball's color barrier in 1947 when he was signed to play for the Brooklyn Dodgers. But he had fought racial inequality before, in a different kind of uniform.

A star running back at UCLA, Robinson was drafted and became a first lieutenant. In 1942, while serving at Camp Hood in Texas, Robinson was charged with insubordination because he refused an order to sit in the back of an army bus.

A white officer claimed Robinson was acting "rather uppity and out to make trouble" for refusing to change his seat and questioned whether he was "trying to start a race riot or something?" Robinson was cleared of the charge at a military hearing. "It wasn't much of a disturbance," he said. "I just exercised my right to sit where I pleased on the camp bus and the driver figured it was his duty to impose Texas segregation laws."

After the war Robinson played in the Negro baseball leagues until April 11, 1947, when he signed a contract with Dodgers manager Branch Rickey. It was such a tradition-shattering move that Robinson wound up on the covers of *Time* and *Life* magazines that season.

Robinson was taunted by white fans; Philadelphia Phillies players yelled racial slurs. But Robinson never fought back. He knew if he did, white owners might never again let a black play in the major leagues. He just kept quiet and played the game to near perfection, earning Rookie of the Year honors.

Robinson is considered one of the greatest to ever play the game. He is also considered a hero for working for racial equality.

war blacks fled the south in great numbers. Lynching and violence by racist groups such as the Ku Klux Klan were still common and Jim Crow segregation laws denied blacks basic civil rights, including the opportunity to vote. The first waves of black movement out of the south had occurred after the Civil War and during World War I. But during the Great Depression, when many blacks became unemployed, thousands had returned to their original homes. This reverse migration did not occur again after World War II.

However, the nation's new racial makeup created racial tensions, including clashes in 1943 between blacks and whites in Detroit, Los Angeles, New York, and other cities. *Newsweek* magazine said the Detroit riot was an example of the "stark explosion of racial hatred burgeoning across the land as war and population shifts threw the races into mounting contact and frictions." [35]

The worst riot began on a hot Sunday afternoon on June 21 at a local Detroit park when whites became upset because they were outnumbered by blacks. Fighting broke out between the races in a crowd of about five thousand on Belles Isle, which lies in the Detroit River. The altercation spilled over into the city of Detroit and by 10:30 P.M. twenty blacks and three whites had been killed. Unrest continued for nearly a week, including looting of local businesses and battles with police. The final death toll was twenty-five blacks and nine whites.

Increased numbers of blacks in the military also created racial problems. But black soldiers and sailors had proved themselves during the war and in 1948 Truman issued an order to integrate the military. This opened up more opportunities in the military for blacks and formally assured them equal rights, something denied them in most areas of civilian life.

Although even blacks in the north still lived in segregated areas after the war, one aspect of life important to Americans did become integrated—the world of sports. In 1946, pro football teams began signing black players for the first time in thirteen years. Blacks had played pro football until 1933. The need for good players after the war ended a "gentleman's agreement" among major league owners not to hire blacks. Kenny Washington, Woody Strode, Marion Motley, and Bill Willis were among the new wave of black stars.

Major league baseball broke the color barrier in 1947, when the Brooklyn Dodgers signed Jackie Robinson. The signing of Robinson, who like other black stars had played in the Negro baseball leagues, had a far greater impact on race relations than the inclusion of blacks in football. Baseball was the era's most popular professional sport. Even GIs at war had followed their teams, debating the merits of the Yankees and Dodgers during lulls in the fighting around the world.

Technology in the Peacetime Economy

The war resulted in major technological advances in many areas, from aviation to new man-made materials like synthetic rubber. In the postwar period, Americans began to reap the benefits of this new knowledge. The new technologies made life easier for many and changed life in a variety of ways.

When the synthetic fiber nylon was introduced in 1940 it was considered a miracle fabric. The postwar years saw the introduction of acetate, acrylic, and polyester fabrics that made "wash and wear" clothes possible. They were not only trendy but

Col. Charles Yeager holds a model of the Bell X-1 experimental airplane he flew in 1947, when he became the first pilot to break the sound barrier. He exceeded 700 miles per hour to create the first sonic boom ever heard.

eliminated hours of ironing.

Technological breakthroughs in aviation opened up the world to Americans by making travel to other countries possible for many more people. After the war, planes were able to fly farther and faster than ever before. On October 14, 1947, Charles Yeager became a national hero when he became the first to break the sound barrier. The sonic boom that echoed across the sky when Yeager topped seven hundred miles an hour in the X-1, a thin-winged, orange experimental plane, signaled a new era in man's mastery over the air.

Radar, a valuable weapon during the war, was now adapted to make air travel safer. Developed by the British, radar was used during the war to spot enemy planes and was a clear advantage in Allied attacks. The new technology was now used to keep track of planes to avoid collisions and to guide pilots to airport landings.

Air travel became an affordable means of transportation for many Americans. The result was that civilian air travel grew from only 2.5 million passengers in 1937 to 21 million in 1947.

Although the results would not be seen for a few years, German research in the V-1 and V-2 rocket programs would help the developing U.S. space program. The Germans developed the rockets late in the war and used the first primitive missiles to bomb London. The United States enlisted German rocket scientists like Wernher von Braun to begin adapting the technology for travel into outer space.

The research and discoveries that led to the atomic bomb were the most important that came out of the war. After the war scientists, who did not entirely understand this new awesome power, began working to find ways in which atomic energy could serve mankind. This new technology was considered so important for the country's future that in 1946 Congress created the Atomic Energy Commission to oversee its development. Eventually, scientists were able to harness the power of the atom to generate electricity, power nuclear submarines, and even heal people when used in new medical equipment.

LPs and Hi-Fis

Technology also changed the way people listened to music. The first commercial long-playing record came out in 1948. Spinning at 33 ⅓ revolutions per minute, LPs allowed people to hear twenty three minutes of uninterrupted music. One LP allowed the listener to hear, without interruption, the music that previously had been

The Rise of Modern Computers

The first modern computers were developed in Great Britian and the United States during World War II as tools to help defeat Germany and Japan.

English mathematician Alan Turing is credited with building the first fully electronic computer, using vacuum tubes instead of mechanical relays. Turing also laid the groundwork for the binary memory system used in all modern computers.

British intelligence began using Turing's computer, nicknamed Colossus, in 1943 to break secret German military codes. A year later Howard Aiken, a Harvard mathematician, helped develop the Mark I electronic computer, which created ballistics tables that improved the accuracy of navy artillery.

In 1946, John W. Mauchly and J. Presper Eckert, engineers at the University of Pennsylvania, created what is considered the first modern general purpose electronic computer. Called ENIAC—Electronic Numerical Integrator and Calculator—it was able to perform 100,000 operations per second, which was two thousand times faster than the Mark I.

ENIAC weighed 30 tons, contained 17,468 vacuum tubes, and had 500 miles of wiring. The invention of the transistor in 1948 helped revolutionize computer development, but it would be decades before the idea of PCs (personal computers) would be workable. The creation of transistor technology also led to many other new products and inventions, including miniaturized radios people could fit in a pocket.

contained on fifteen smaller records, which spun at 78 rpm, that had been the standard phonograph discs since before the turn of the century.

The year 1948 also saw the introduction of stereophonic sound, which gave records a lush new quality termed "high fidelity." In the next decade people no longer bought record players, they bought "hi-fis," and assembled audio systems capable of more accurate recording and higher volume than ever. It was a revolution for the ear and the music industry.

The New American Dream

The first few years after World War II were among the happiest in U.S. history. Servicemen relieved to have survived the war were welcomed home as heroes. They returned to a nation with a newly vibrant economy strong enough to offer them more job opportunities than they could have imagined a few years earlier. Anxious to make up for the years of their youth wasted on war they went to school, got jobs, and began their own businesses. Millions married and started families.

Denied the luxuries of life for so many years by the Great Depression and the war, Americans went on a buying binge. The new prosperity reshaped the American Dream, now defined in part as a house in the suburbs, that trendy new place to live which offered so many people their first chance at home ownership. The house had to have a neatly manicured lawn and a garage with not one but two cars. Their homes quickly filled with new technological gadgets to make life easier and more entertaining, from appliances to television sets.

The war had made America a richer, more powerful nation than ever before. And Americans began to enjoy themselves as never before.

Chapter Six

A young couple does the "Big Apple," just one of the dance crazes that swept the nation in the forties. Big bands punched out popular tunes that kept American youths dancing and singing through World War II.

Popular Culture: From Jack Benny to Howdy Doody

At the end of World War II more American homes had radios than bathtubs, some 30 million of them. It was a form of entertainment and information, inexpensive and available at the flick of a switch, that helped millions of people survive the tough times of the Great Depression and the war.

Radio shows featured the corny jokes of Bob Hope, Jack Benny, and

In 1942 a family in Provincetown, Massachusetts, gathers around the family radio, the center of entertainment in every American home. Radio had shows for everyone in the family—boxing, soap operas, thrilling adventure shows, and popular dance tunes.

ventriloquist Edgar Bergen, whose wooden partners Charlie McCarthy and Mortimer Snerd were as beloved as their creator. Listeners enjoyed the swinging sounds of the Glenn Miller and Tommy Dorsey Orchestras and huddled around their radios for live broadcasts of heavyweight champion Joe Louis knocking out yet another challenger. Audiences tuned in to soap operas, mysteries, and escapist fare like "the thrilling adventures of Superman." The "fireside chats" of Franklin D.

Roosevelt brought the president into their homes for the first time.

Radio was often called "theater of the mind." Huddled around their sets, listeners had to use their imagination to visualize the stories that were being narrated and acted out in studios thousands of miles away. People were fascinated with soap opera serials like *Ma Perkins* and *The Guiding Light* and the adventures of *Superman*, *The Lone Ranger*, and *The Shadow*. Listeners painted their own mental pictures of their favorite characters right down to Silver, the snow-white horse the Lone Ranger rode as he battled villains in the Old West.

Radio brought world events to people with a new sense of immediacy and urgency. Just a few decades earlier, Americans might have had to wait days or even weeks before they could read newspaper stories about events of importance. But radio described history as it was happening, even in far-away places. It was the medium that informed the nation that Pearl Harbor had been attacked, that President Roosevelt had died, that a new, unbelievably powerful weapon called an atomic bomb had been used to defeat Japan.

Journalist Edward R. Murrow once said, "I, for one, do not believe that a people who have the world brought into their homes by a radio can remain indifferent to what happens in the world." [36]

Radio Shows

Radio had something for everybody.

Comedy fans who tuned in to shows starring Jack Benny, Bob Hope, Fred Allen, and George Burns and Gracie Allen were treated to whimsical story lines and snappy one-liners that kept the nation laughing through difficult times. The humor was simple and often corny by present-day standards.

An example of radio humor were the jokes built around Jack Benny's image as a cheapskate. When Benny was held up, the robber told him: "Your money or your life." After a long period of silence, the robber again issued his ultimatum—only to hear Benny say, "I'm thinking, I'm thinking!"

Soap operas like *The Romance of Helen Trent*, *Ma Perkins*, and *The Guiding Light* fascinated women. Shows always ended with tag lines like "Be sure to listen tomorrow to the next episode of *Our Gal Sunday*" to keep audiences tuning in daily. The soap operas reflected World War II; Ma Perkins, lead character in a show that ran for twenty-seven years, had a son who was killed in the war.

Radio also offered mystery and horror theater to thrill and frighten audiences, and radio hosts dared their listeners to turn off the lights while listening. "The seed of crime bears bitter fruit. Crime does not pay! The Shadow knows": Those lines were part of the opening to *The Shadow*, about a mysterious crime fighter with the power to "cloud men's minds." Though the Shadow was a hero, he was a spooky, sinister character. His eerie laugh, supposed to scare the meanest criminal, did the same to many listeners.

Musical shows played records and featured bands in live performances from famous nightclubs. Sports fans listened to heavyweight fights and football and baseball games. Radio also brought news to people faster and more dramatically than ever before.

He was right. His own dramatic reports from London during the Blitz had helped change the nation's perceptions about whether it should fight in World War II.

Radio had a tremendous power to entertain, inform, and captivate its audience. And with the entire nation tuning in to the same shows, music, and news, radio even began to eliminate some of the regional differences that had divided the nation's citizens. Listeners from Hoboken, New Jersey, to Honolulu, Hawaii, developed a shared understanding about the world around them. They also began to understand each other a little bit better. Radio helped unite the forty-eight states in a way no other medium ever had.

Although radio was a vital part of daily life in the '40s, it was only one element of the popular culture of the times, embodied in the music people listened to, movies they watched, books they read, clothes they wore, the celebrities who became their heroes, and the jokes they laughed at. And in the decade's final years television debuted as a powerful new medium, one that would profoundly change modern society.

Music

In the '40s Americans listened to many different kinds of music, including country, blues, jazz, and classical. But the most popular was the dance music played by the big bands, whose leaders were as well known as rock stars are today. Music lovers were able to "swing and sway" to the bands of Glenn Miller, Benny Goodman, Tommy Dorsey, Duke Ellington, Les Brown, Kay Kyser, and Count Basie. When the bands toured the country, thousands of fans turned out to listen and "cut a rug," the '40s slang term for dancing.

The nation enjoyed romantic tunes like "Don't Sit Under the Apple Tree with Anyone Else but Me," a plea from one young lover to another that was especially poignant to young soldiers far from home, and swinging big band dance tunes like "Chattanooga Choo Choo" and "In the Mood."

The big bands were really big, with twenty or more musicians in saxophone, trumpet, trombone, and clarinet sections. The bands were rounded out by piano, bass, and drum players and most featured popular vocalists. Many bandleaders also played instruments—Benny Goodman the clarinet, Harry James the trumpet, and Glenn Miller the trombone.

Whether they performed on their own or as part of a band, all-girl singing groups were very popular in the '40s and the Andrews Sisters'

The Glenn Miller Orchestra was the most popular big band in the forties. Miller, on the bottom level of the stage playing the trombone, died in an airplane crash during the war while entertaining troops in Europe.

recording of "Boogie Woogie Bugle Boy of Company B" was one of the biggest hits of World War II.

Many different types of songs caught the public's fancy: "When I Wish upon a Star," the sentimental song from the Walt Disney movie *Pinocchio*; "Remember Pearl Harbor" and "Praise the Lord and Pass the Ammunition," two of many war-themed songs, the latter supposedly inspired by a phrase uttered by a chaplain at Pearl Harbor; and "Mule Train," a country tune that featured the crack of a bullwhip. Broadway shows contributed hits like "This Is the Army," and "Oklahoma."

Wacky novelty songs were big hits in the '40s. The nonsensical lyrics of "Marzy Doats," caught the nation's fancy. "I Came, I Saw, I Conga'd" was inspired by the craze over the dance of the same name. Latin music was popular, including, "Down Argentine Way," performed by Carmen Miranda. A dancer and singer, Miranda became famous for the elaborate headpieces she wore, which included flowers and

Frank Sinatra, seen in this 1942 publicity photo, was the forties' most popular male singer and the first teen idol. When he sang, Sinatra thrilled teenage girls so much that they screamed themselves hoarse and fainted away.

pieces of fruit. "Rudolph the Red-Nosed Reindeer" by cowboy star Gene Autry and "All I Want for Christmas Is My Two Front Teeth" are modern Christmas favorites first recorded in the '40s.

Music of all sorts was so popular that by 1946 Americans were buying ten times as many records as a decade earlier. RCA and Decca both sold more than 100 million records that year. The jukebox industry also became big business. Although it only cost a nickel to play a tune, by the end of the decade 400,000 jukeboxes were raking in $80 million a year.

The Rise of Youth Culture

In the early years of the decade Bing Crosby was the nation's most popular singer because of hits like "White Christmas" and a host of romantic ballads. But during the war Crosby was replaced as the nation's singing idol by Frank Sinatra, the skinny crooner nicknamed "Swoonatra" for his effect on teenage girls. His solo career began in 1942, after successful years with Tommy Dorsey.

The Sinatra craze was so powerful it sparked a new type of teenage behavior from "bobby-soxers." Easily identifiable by their turned-down ankle socks, baggy sweaters, and long, pleated skirts, bobby-soxers were teenage girls who mobbed Sinatra wherever he went. They screamed mindlessly when he performed, many actually fainting from the excitement of hearing their favorite singer.

An example of the bobby-soxer phenomenon occurred on October 12, 1944, when Sinatra performed before a sellout crowd of thirty-six hundred at the Paramount Theater in New York. More than ten thousand screaming

These young girls were fortunate enough to get tickets to the Frank Sinatra concert in New York City on October 12, 1944. Thousands of fans who failed to get tickets for the show came anyway just to be near their idol.

girls were still outside trying to buy tickets while another twenty thousand were mobbing nearby Times Square just trying to get close to their idol. It took seven hundred riot police to restore order. Incidents like this caused one member of Congress to denounce Sinatra as "one of the prime instigators of juvenile delinquency in America."[37] It was an attitude that would surface again a decade later when adults complained that rock 'n' roll stars such as Elvis Presley were corrupting America's youth.

The bobby-sox craze, however, is just one example of how the war transformed the status and lifestyle of teenagers. The major change in the status of teenagers was that more of them worked, which gave them more freedom and spending money than ever before. By 1943 almost 3 million boys and girls were working on farms and in factories, including a half-million in defense plants. The result was that 1.25 million students dropped out of school during the war, prompting the National Education

Association to issue a plea to teenagers to stay in school. Many of those who did were so tired from working, they fell asleep in class.

Before the new postwar prosperity, teens had mostly been restricted to low-paying, part-time jobs, and most of the money they made went to support the family. But teenagers now had their own money to spend and became an important new segment of the consumer economy.

Teens spent their newfound wealth on records, clothing, and recreation. Recognizing teenagers as a distinct new consumer group, advertisers began aiming marketing campaigns at them. *Seventeen* and other magazines for teens were suddenly popular and newspapers like the *Chicago Daily News* ran columns on "Teen News" and "Teen Views."

The result was the emergence in the '40s, for the first time, of a distinct youth subculture that would become even more influential in the future in shaping popular culture in America. People ages thirteen to nineteen were no longer simply growing youths, they were "teenagers"—a phrase that itself did not become commonly used until this period in U.S. history.

Teenagers went to concerts and dances, listened to music on the radio, flocked to the movies, and attended parties at each other's homes. Slumber parties for girls also became popular. One of the most popular gathering places for teens was the ice cream shop, where they could dance to jukebox music while slurping down ice cream treats and sodas.

"Jukebox Saturday Night," one of the most popular songs of the period, described a night out for teens this way:

Moppin' up soda pop rickeys,
To our heart's delight,
Dancin' to swingeroo quickies,
Jukebox Saturday night.

Teens danced to the same big band tunes as their parents. But during the war they adopted the jitterbug, which first appeared in the late '30s, as their favorite dance. The jitterbug was an exuberant, creative form of expression that was more frenzied athleticism than rhythmic dance. It included "air steps" in which male and even female dancers lifted each other off the floor. Men tossed their partners in the air and swung them around their bodies and even between their legs. It was not a dance for the faint of heart.

Clothing styles became more important to teens, who became rigidly conformist in the way they dressed, adopting a uniform style that set them apart from adults. When girls were not wearing their bobby-sox and pleated skirts, they often put on blue jeans that were rolled up to just below the knee and often decorated with painted hearts, horses, and other figures. Girls also favored knee-high striped football socks and men's shirts or blouses with the tails hanging out. On dates they liked to wear formal dresses with jewelry and high-heeled shoes.

Boys generally wore jeans that were rolled up at the ankle to show off their fashionable white socks and loafers. Shirttails were never tucked in. They donned suits or sport coats and ties for big dates. Long hair was in for girls, who copied hairstyles of their favorite movie actresses. Some boys began wearing their hair longer in the back, a forerunner of the "ducktail" look of the next decade.

An extreme style during the war was the "zoot suit," which Sinatra helped make popular. The look was highlighted by its "drape shape." The coat had oversized, padded shoulders that narrowed to a tightly tucked-in waist before flaring out again. It also had wide lapels with what was known as a "reet pleat." The pants were high waisted, cut full in the thigh and tapering to wrap tightly around the ankle in what was called a "peg leg." Zoot suiters also wore large, floppy

The jitterbug, with its athletic moves and frenetic pace, was a dance for the young and fearless. Older people could only shake their heads at the foolish antics, much as these jitterbuggers probably did years later when their own children began dancing to rock 'n' roll music.

hats, gaudy ties, and a mandatory key chain, a long length of metal that began at the belt and often looped below the knee.

Zoot suits were most popular with black and Hispanic youths, but the look spread across the nation. However, the suits caused a riot in May 1942 in Los Angeles, where most zoot suiters were Mexican youths. Zoot suiters and sailors got into a brawl at a dance hall that spilled over into several nights of fighting between the two groups. Although the clashes

The zoot suit was the height of fashion, but it was not for everybody. Note the hip (for that era, at least) way they are greeting each other by sliding the underside of their outstretched hands across each other's palms instead of shaking hands.

reflected racial tensions rather than style issues, the Los Angeles City Council temporarily banned the wearing of zoot suits.

It's Howdy Doody Time!

When Buffalo Bob asked, "Hey, kids, what time is it?" tens of millions of youngsters in the late '40s had the answer. It was time to watch the *Howdy Doody* show. It was also time for an entire nation to be captivated by a new form of entertainment that emerged in the postwar years and would redefine American culture more powerfully than

any other medium.

The technology to broadcast pictures and sound had existed since the early 1920s. But the evolution and growth of this startling new medium was held back by the Great Depression and World War II. Now the postwar boom economy was the ideal catalyst.

By the end of the war there were fewer than seven thousand TV sets in the nation and only nine broadcast stations. The stations were located mostly in eastern states and broadcast only a handful of programs on a very limited schedule, mainly in large cities. But on October 8, 1945, the government lifted its ban on construction of new stations. The result was an explosion of new outlets that were consolidated into networks that could beam shows to most of the nation.

The growth of television was slowed at first by the unavailability of sets, which cost $700, an astronomical sum at the time. In the first eight months of 1946 factories produced only 225 sets, with tiny, six-inch screens, but the number rose sharply after that. In the month of September 3,242 sets were produced and in May 1947 nearly 8,700. Cash rich and hungry for this new form of entertainment, Americans bought TVs as fast as they came off the assembly lines. By

1949 Americans were taking home 100,000 sets a week.

In a newspaper ad on January 5, 1948, announcing its new network season, the National Broadcasting Company (NBC) declared the new year "marks TV's appearance as a major force. The greatest means of

Kids' TV Shows

One of the first stars of television had red hair and freckles. He wore a cowboy shirt and boots and always sported a neckerchief. He also had strings attached to his feet and legs.

Howdy Doody was a marionette and the star of the pioneer children's show *Howdy Doody*, which debuted December 27, 1947, and ran for thirteen years, televised every afternoon just as kids were coming home from school. Along with other children's shows, it helped the youngsters of the first TV generation fall in love with the brand-new medium.

Other early favorite kids' shows were *Kukla, Fran, and Ollie*, which featured puppets instead of marionettes; *Captain Video and His Rangers*, television's first series with a science fiction theme; and *Winchell and Mahoney*, starring ventriloquist Paul Winchell and his dummy, Jerry Mahoney. Mahoney had a best friend with an appropriate name for a dummy —Knucklehead Smith.

But Howdy Doody was by far the most popular with children. Buffalo Bob Smith was the adult host of the show, which included cartoons and film shorts as well as story lines involving Howdy and other residents of Doodyville. Dilly - Dally was Howdy's best friend, Phineas T. Bluster the resident villain, and Clarabell the clown a mischief maker who communicated by honking his horn and

Buffalo Bob Smith and Howdy Doody were two of the early stars of television. The kids' show named after the red-haired, freckled marionette introduced the new medium to the first generation of youngsters that would grow up watching television.

squirted people with water from a bottle he carried.

Many of the early children's shows had studio audiences; the group of kids on *Howdy Doody* was dubbed the "peanut gallery."

Forties Slang

Every era produces a unique jargon—new words or phrases that catch people's fancy and sometimes set the tone of the times. Here are some from the forties.

barber: to gossip.
brown cow: chocolate milk.
bucket: a large, old car.
cut a rug: dance.
drugstore cowboy: a teenager who spent hours at drugstore soda fountains.
duck soup: any task that is easy to do.
GI: a soldier, short for government issue.
Geronimo: the yell soldiers gave when they jumped from planes; also used to express excitement in other activities.
gobbledygook: nonsense.
Jeep: name for the four-wheel-drive vehicle first used in World War II.
jeet: Did you eat?
Jill: a girlfriend.
Joe: term for an average guy; also GI Joe for a soldier and Joe College for a college student.
mothball: a serious student.
nervous pudding: Jell-O.
on the hoof: meat that is very rare.
orchard: a baseball park.
pancake turner: a disc jockey.
put on the dog: to dress in fancy clothes.
red lead: ketchup.
reet: excellent or perfect.
Snow White: 7-Up.
suds: root beer.
takes a flower: served with onions.
white cow: a vanilla milkshake.
wreck a pair: scrambled eggs.

mass communication in the world is with us." [38] In 1948 there were only four networks—the American Broadcasting Company (ABC), Columbia Broadcasting System (CBS), NBC, and DuMont, which later failed—that broadcast shows over thirty-seven stations in a twenty-two-state area on the East Coast. But television was quickly becoming available to an entire nation.

In its infancy the new medium depended on news, sports, comedies, old movies, and children's shows like *Howdy Doody*. Many of the first TV shows were transplants from radio such as *The Lone Ranger*, *Ted Mack's Original Amateur Hour*, a weekly contest for singers and other performers, and *The Goldbergs*, a comedy about Jewish immigrants.

Many of TV's first stars were also recycled from radio and other forms of entertainment. One was Milton Berle, a vaudeville comedian who had never been a big star. But his comedy-variety show in 1948 became one of the biggest hits of early television, earning him the nickname "Mr. Television" and endearing "Uncle Miltie" to the first generation of television viewers.

Berle, a slapstick comedian who was not above dressing as a woman to get laughs, became so popular that people began staying home at night so they would not miss his antics. Shows like his made television part of everyday life for Americans, something they felt they could not do without. It began to change the way people lived.

Sports

Sports were an important part of life in the '40s. Even World War II travel restrictions and the loss of stars to military duty, from heavyweight champion Joe Louis to baseball star Ted Williams, could not dim their popularity.

President Roosevelt felt sports were so necessary to morale that in early 1942 he approved the continuation of professional baseball, the reigning national passion, during the war. Until his announcement, the status of baseball and other pro sports leagues was uncertain, subject to wartime interruption. "I honestly felt it would be best for the country to keep baseball going," the president said. "[It was] a definite recreational asset to at least 20 million of their fellow citizens." [39]

Joe DiMaggio, one of the greatest players of all time, takes a swing during the 1941 season when he hit in a record fifty-six straight games. He earned the nickname "Joltin' Joe" for his hitting prowess.

In 1941 baseball fans joyously watched as Joe DiMaggio of the New York Yankees slugged his way to a record fifty-six-game hitting streak and Ted Williams of the Boston Red Sox batted .406. More than a half-century later, DiMaggio's record still stood and no one had batted .400 again.

Millions of returning GIs, hungry for sports, had an endless appetite for boxing, football, baseball, and just about any other sporting event. Television helped satisfy that desire and in turn boosted the popularity of sports even further.

In the fall of 1948 the National Football league (NFL) became the first

The Olympic flame is rekindled in London in 1948 in the first Olympic Games after the war. Because the Olympic Games could not be held in 1940 and 1944, the 1948 event was welcomed by the nations of the world as a sign of returning normalcy.

Television exposure contributed to the formation in 1946 of a rival to the NFL, the eight-team All-America Football Conference. The leagues waged a fight for players coming out of the service, escalating salaries in the process. But in 1949 the leagues merged, with the Cleveland Browns, San Francisco 49ers, and Baltimore Colts joining the NFL.

Pro basketball began in 1947 with creation of the Basketball Association of America (BAA). The Philadelphia Warriors won the first season championship, beating the Chicago Stars in a five-game series. In 1950 the BAA merged with the National Basketball League, a minor league that played mostly in the Midwest, to form today's National Basketball Association (NBA).

World War II contributed a tradition to professional sports that still exists today—playing the national anthem at the start of a game. The song served as a patriotic reminder to sports fans that a war was going on.

The Olympic Games

The 1948 Olympics were the first held since 1936, when black American athletes like Jesse Owens had shattered the German myth of Aryan supremacy in the Summer Games in Berlin. Owens, who won four gold medals, never forgot the strange quality of the

sport with weekly network coverage. The first television broadcast of a baseball game had occurred way back in 1939, when only a few thousand people had TV sets, but now baseball too became very popular on TV. Pro wrestling was a huge hit in the early years of television.

Berlin games: "I remember Hitler coming in with his entourage and the storm troopers standing shoulder to shoulder like an iron fence. Then came the roar of 'Heil Hitler' from ten thousand throats and all those arms outstretched [in a Nazi salute]. It was eerie and frightening."[40]

In 1948 participating nations viewed the Olympics as a celebration of worldwide peace. During the Winter Games in St. Moritz, Switzerland, eighteen-year-old Dick Button became the first American to win gold in figure skating. The Harvard freshman revolutionized the sport, introducing athleticism as a component by becoming the first skater to do two full turns in the air during a jump.

The ruins of buildings destroyed in the Blitz were a stark backdrop to the Summer Games in London. Harrison Dillard, a black infantryman in Italy during the war, won the hundred-meter dash and seventeen-year-old Bob Mathias became the youngest American gold medalist by winning the decathlon.

Books

Wartime restrictions on travel made Americans turn to leisure activities they could pursue at home. They played card and board games and devoured books as reading became a national passion. Paperback books, introduced at the beginning of the decade, sold for only a quarter and made books available to more people. Shortages of paper helped popularize the new format. The '40s saw the rise of commerial book clubs, which made best-sellers available more widely and inexpensively than ever before. More than fifty such clubs sold 3 million books a month.

People read mysteries like *Ten Little Indians* by Agatha Christie and historical novels such as *The Robe* by Lloyd C. Douglas. Hard-boiled detectives like Philip Marlowe solved crimes in novels by Raymond Chandler while Zane Grey and others churned out westerns, which were among the most popular of books.

A host of novels depicted the war. Considered the finest war novel was Norman Mailer's *The Naked and the Dead*, published in 1948. Mailer had fought in the South Pacific and his gritty, dramatic account of combat was a best-seller.

Making People Happy

Movies, radio, television, music, sports, and books all have one thing in common—the ability to make people happy and forget their troubles, if only for a little while. And during the

Comic Books

Comic book superheroes went to war with Germany before the United States did. The '40s was the golden age of superheroes thanks to Superman, who debuted in 1938. He was followed by Batman, Aquaman, Wonder Woman, Captain Marvel, and other heroes with special powers.

The February 1940 issue of Marvel Comics featured a story about the Submariner, who lived in the sea and had superpowers. He started fighting the Germans because they had invaded his sea world and were killing marine life.

Many comic book heroes fought during World War II, but not Superman, who was declared 4-F, the designation for recruits physically unfit for duty. The caped crusader from the planet Krypton failed his eye test when he accidentally used his X-ray vision to read the eye chart in the next room. Publishers thought it would mock the war effort to put Superman, who would have been able to win the war by himself in a single day, in uniform.

One hero, Captain America, personified wartime patriotism. Army scientists injected Steve Rogers, a scrawny 4-F, with a secret formula that gave him superpowers to fight the Nazis. His star-studded costume was red, white, and blue—making him look like a walking flag with bulging muscles. Youngsters who joined Captain America's Sentinels of Liberty Club had to promise to collect newspapers, magazines, cardboard, boxes, and cartons. He proclaimed: "You can do your part in winning this war by joining the wastepaper drive!"

Comic strip characters in newspapers also went to war. Buzz Sawyer was a navy pilot and Joe Palooka, a heavyweight boxing champion, joined the infantry. *Terry and the Pirates*, an adventure series set in China, featured battles against the Japanese.

difficult years of World War II, Americans needed them greatly.

Young couples danced away their cares and worries to a popular tune by Glenn Miller. People spent hours in darkened theaters, watching flickering images on a silver screen create another sort of reality, one that could take them away from their problems. Books, board games, and other pursuits helped people forget, if only briefly, the terrible things that were happening around the world.

Many elements of American popular culture help people achieve one of the most basic human needs—to be happy even when life is difficult. Thus something as trivial as a comic strip that can elicit a smile or chuckle can have powerful value in people's lives. It was that way during the '40s. It is still that way today.

Chapter Seven

An obviously ailing President Franklin D. Roosevelt sits between English prime minister Winston Churchill (left), and Soviet Union leader Joseph Stalin during the Yalta Conference. Decisions made at this important 1945 meeting of the Big Three set the stage for the cold war.

The Cold War

When World War II ended, the United States was militarily and economically the most powerful nation in the world. And America, which in the past had followed its isolationist leanings by keeping its distance from other nations, was finally ready to assume a significant role in world affairs.

The United States took the lead in establishing the United Nations, offering it a permanent home in New York. It supplied aid to millions of war refugees and helped countries devastated by the fighting rebuild their shattered homelands, including its former enemies Germany and Japan. The United States, which since the 1920s had restricted immigration, opened its arms to war refugees. The Displaced Persons Act of 1948 allowed more than 400,000 Europeans to enter the country.

Perhaps the saddest fact of the postwar era is that peace proved elusive. Germany and Japan had been defeated, but the United States and the Soviet Union soon emerged as the principal players in a new conflict, one that would continue for more than four decades.

"The refusal of the Soviet Union to work with its wartime allies for world recovery and world peace is the most bitter disappointment of our time. . . . The cleavage that exists is not between the Soviet Union and the United States. It is between the Soviet Union and the rest of the world," [41] President Truman said in 1948.

This clash of ideologies was called the cold war because it stopped short of overt military action. The weapons the two sides wielded were diplomatic measures, propaganda, intelligence networks, economic and military aid to other countries, and the threat of nuclear war.

For the United States, the cold war was a fight against communism, a totalitarian political philosophy and form of government in which the state owns and controls all segments of the economy. America's leaders and citizens believed communism was a threat to democracy and to capitalism, which is based on private ownership of property and a free market econo-my. Americans believed that democracy and capitalism would allow everyone an equal chance to be successful in their lives.

The Soviet Union, on the other hand, believed that capitalism was evil. Communists said capitalism held average workers in a form of economic bondage, denying them opportunities while allowing the rich owners of the means of production to amass even more wealth. Communism advocated, more in theory than in practice, the equal distribution of goods and state ownership of the means of production. This message was popular in impoverished countries, especially nations whose economies had not become industrialized.

The battle lines for this new conflict began to be drawn in the final months of the war at a place called Yalta.

The Cold War Begins

In February 1945 President Franklin D. Roosevelt met with British prime minister Winston Churchill and Soviet leader Joseph Stalin at Yalta, a resort city on the Black Sea in Russia. The Yalta Conference is considered the starting point for the cold war.

Germany was on the verge of defeat and Roosevelt, Churchill, and Stalin—known as the "Big Three"—

were in Yalta to decide how to organize Europe after the war. At the center of the talks was the fate of Poland and Germany.

The Soviet Union wanted a communist postwar Poland; Roosevelt and Churchill wanted a democratic government. At Yalta they agreed to let Poles choose for themselves in a free election. They also agreed that other countries under German occupation, such as Bulgaria and Romania, would be allowed to elect new leaders.

Stalin wanted Germany, a foe of Russia for centuries, dismantled so it could never again pose a threat. The United States and Great Britian wanted to purge Germany of Nazism but argued for its continued existence as a nation under a democratic form of rule. The compromise reached at Yalta was that after the war, Germany would be divided into four sectors. The United States, Great Britian, France, and the Soviet Union would each have jurisdiction over one sector, but Germany would be under the overall control of a council made up of all four powers. Eventually the four sectors would be reunited into one nation.

Stalin also agreed to join the fight against Japan in return for

The United Nations

"We seek peace—enduring peace. More than an end to war, we want an end to the beginnings of all wars—yes, an end to this brutal, inhuman, and thoroughly impractical method of settling the differences between governments." Those words were part of the last message Franklin Roosevelt wrote before his death.

Throughout the war, the United States had felt establishment of a successor to the failed League of Nations would be the key to ensuring world peace. The name United Nations (UN) was first used at a meeting in Washington, D.C., January 1, 1942. Representatives of twenty-six nations signed the Declaration of the United Nations that day and pledged to join it after the war.

From August 21 to October 7, 1944, at the Dumbarton Oaks Conference in Washington, D.C., participating nations agreed on general principles for the new organization. At the Yalta Conference the following year the United States, Great Britain, the Soviet Union, France, and China—collectively known as the "Big Five"—worked out an organizational plan.

In April 1945, representatives of fifty nations met in San Francisco to found the United Nations and approved its charter. Although the fledgling UN had very little power in its first few years, it has served since then to bring nations together to talk over and resolve problems that in the past would have led to war.

Soviet Union leader Joseph Stalin began World War II on the side of Germany and finished it fighting with the Allies. Stalin felt the millions of Soviet soldiers who were wounded or died to defeat Germany gave his country the right to take control of a large part of Europe after the war.

concessions in Asia. The Soviets were promised some small islands near Japan, joint control over the railroads of Manchuria in China, and special privileges in two key seaports in that area, Dairen and Port Arthur.

Roosevelt agreed to the concessions because he felt Russia's help was needed to win the war in the Pacific. The conference predated the comple-

tion of the atomic bomb; at that time, the Allies calculated it would take another year of bloody fighting to subdue Japan, and Roosevelt felt Russian support would reduce the loss of American lives.

At Yalta the three Allied powers also agreed to join a new world organization called the United Nations, which would be the successor to the League of Nations. This last promise was the only one the Soviets honored. Russia never allowed free elections in Poland or other nations. It did not allow Germany to be reunited. Instead, the Soviet Union used the postwar weakness of many nations to expand its territory.

Soviet Expansion

At war's end the Soviet Union occupied Eastern and Central Europe east of a rough line extending from the western Baltic Sea in the north to the Adriatic Sea at Trieste in the south. This line was about 110 miles west of Berlin, Germany's capital. In Asia it controlled Manchuria and North Korea. The Soviets, who had suffered millions more deaths and casualties than any other nation in the war, felt they had earned the right to keep this new territory. Russia sought control of countries like Poland, Hungary, and Czechoslovakia on the grounds that it needed a buffer against possible future invasion from the rest of Europe.

Russia installed a provisional government in Poland that took its orders from Moscow. Bulgaria, Romania, Albania, Czechoslovakia, and Hungary all came under Soviet domination.

In March 1946 in a speech in Fulton, Missouri, Winston Churchill eloquently defined the borders of the cold war: "From Stettin in the Baltic to Trieste in the Adriatic an iron curtain has descended across the continent."[42] The Iron Curtain referred to the Soviet guns, tanks, and airplanes that confined millions of Eastern Europeans. Churchill also warned that "Communist parties or fifth columns [in European nations] constitute a growing challenge and peril to Christian civilization." [43]

Communists were also trying to win control of countries in Asia. When the war ended, the Soviet Union controlled part of Korea. The country was partitioned, much as Germany had been, and the Soviet Union set up a Communist government in North Korea. South Korea became a democracy. The halves were eventually to be reunited, but mounting antagonism between the two,

Russian women scavenge in the ruins of Stalingrad in 1942. By the end of World War II, the fighting had destroyed huge sections of Europe, leaving people nowhere to live and no resources with which to work and make a living.

backed by the two superpowers, erupted into the Korean War in 1950.

The Truman Doctrine

By January 1946 President Truman had grown skeptical of Soviet intentions. He realized the USSR would not honor postwar agreements concerning

President Harry S Truman (left) meets with Secretary of War Henry Stimson. Truman's decision to keep communism from spreading to other nations, called the Truman Doctrine, helped set the United States on a course of conflict that lasted for fifty years.

Europe and was bent on taking whatever land it could. "Unless Russia is faced with an iron fist and strong language, another war is in the making," he wrote in a letter. "Only one language do they understand—'How many divisions have you?' I do not think we should play compromise any longer." He also wrote, "I'm tired of babying the Soviets." [44]

A year later, on March 12, 1947, Truman set the United States on an irrevocable course of confrontation with the Soviet Union, which at the time was trying to win control of Greece and Turkey by supporting armed groups trying to overthrow their governments. In a speech to Congress, Truman asked for economic aid to bolster the legitimate governments of Greece and Turkey against a Soviet takeover.

In what became known as the Truman Doctrine, the president pledged the United States would work to contain communism around the world:

> I believe that it must be the policy of the United States to support free peoples who are resisting attempted subjugation by armed minorities or by outside pressures. I believe that we must assist free people to work out their own destinies in their own way. I believe that our help should be primarily through economic and financial aid which is essential to economic stability and orderly political processes. [45]

Congress quickly granted his request for $400 million in aid (the figure eventually rose to $700 million) for Mediterranean countries, most of it for Greece and Turkey.

Part of the rationale for the Truman Doctrine was provided by George F. Kennan, a foreign policy adviser and Soviet expert serving at the time in the U.S. embassy in Moscow. He had sent Washington a

Harry S Truman

Harry S Truman was an unlikely successor to Franklin Delano Roosevelt.

Truman grew up on a farm, fought in World War I as an artillery officer, and in 1921 went into politics. In 1934 he was elected to the U.S. Senate. He had only a high school education and his homespun philosophy—phrases like "The buck stops here" and "If you can't stand the heat, get out of the kitchen"—appealed to average Americans. They especially appreciated his willingness to accept responsibility for his actions.

During World War II, Truman chaired a committee that investigated waste in defense spending. He saved taxpayers hundreds of millions of dollars by uncovering fraudulent spending on projects and pinpointing outdated and inefficient methods in defense work. It was this work that won him the vice presidential nomination.

A short, plainspoken man of modest means born in Independence, Missouri, Truman contrasted sharply with the elegant, eloquent, wealthy Roosevelt. But within a few months after becoming president, Truman had to make one of the most difficult decisions ever faced by a chief executive—whether to use the atomic bomb on Japan.

A senator from Missouri until elected vice president in 1944, Truman did not even learn about the top secret Manhattan Project, sponsor of atomic weapon research, until a week after he became president. Within months he ordered the use of atomic bombs on Hiroshima and Nagasaki.

"As president of the United States, I had the fateful responsibility of deciding whether or not to use the atom bomb for the first time," he said in 1948. "It was the hardest decision I ever had to make. But the president cannot duck hard problems—he cannot pass the buck."

As president, Truman oversaw the successful postwar conversion of the economy, helped shape America's new role as a world power, and stood up to the Soviet Union as the United States slipped into the cold war. Elected president in his own right in 1948, he declined to run for reelection in 1952.

lengthy analysis in which he recommended as the only way to stop the spread of communism "a policy of firm containment designed to confront the Russians with unalterable counterforce at every point where they show signs of encroaching upon the interests of a peaceful and stable world." [46] This policy of containment formed the foundation for the Truman Doctrine and remained the guiding philosophy of the cold war.

By the spring of 1947, most of Europe was on the verge of economic and social collapse as the devastating effects of World War II. Communist groups controlled by the Soviet Union were making gains in France, Italy, Germany, and other countries in a general atmosphere of political unrest;

Communists seized control of Czechoslovakia in a 1948 coup.

The United States felt it had to find a way to strengthen the European democracies. The weapon, again, would be foreign aid.

Secretary of State George C. Marshall proposed what came to be known as the Marshall Plan. Signed into law by President Truman on April 3, 1948, this massive program of postwar aid to Europe funneled more than $12 billion to sixteen Western European nations over a four-year period. The Economic Cooperation Administration (ECA) was set up to administer the program. ECA reported in 1951 that in countries that had received aid, overall production increased 37 percent, agricultural production rose 25 percent, and steel production nearly doubled.

The cold war also altered the way the United States and other Allies treated Germany and Japan. Postwar occupations of the two enemy nations by Allied forces purged them of the Nazi and militaristic leaders held responsible for World War II and helped them establish democratic governments. The United States was the sole occupation force in Japan.

With Communists making gains in Europe and Asia, the two former enemy nations became valuable allies

in the fight against communism. In a speech January 6, 1948, in San Francisco, Secretary of the Army Kenneth Royall explained the new role Japan was expected to play in world affairs: "We're building in Japan a self-sufficient democracy, strong enough and stable enough to support itself and at the same time serve as a deterrent against any other totalitarian threats which might thereafter arise in the Far East." [47]

To support these new alliances the United States poured billions of dollars in aid into Japanese and German reconstruction, and both nations emerged within a few decades as two of the strongest, richest nations in the world. Marshall funds to European nations and aid to Germany and Japan renewed the economies in all of those countries, gave people new hope for the future, and stabilized their democratic governments.

In addition to wielding economic power, the United States invested heavily in military preparedness. In 1948 Congress approved the nation's first peacetime draft because, for the first time in its history, it was deemed necessary to maintain a large army even though the country was not at war. Before long the United States had to deploy its military to deal with the Soviets.

The Berlin Airlift

The increased tensions between the United States and Soviet Union erupted into a showdown involving Berlin, the former capital of Germany. Although the city of Berlin was more than a hundred miles inside the Soviet zone, it had been divided into four sectors controlled by the United States, Britain, France, and Russia and remained strategically important to all four powers.

In June 1948 the three Western nations instituted currency reform in Germany that was seen as a prelude to reunification of the nation. The Soviet Union, which wanted to keep Germany weak and divided, retaliated by blockading Berlin. It cut off overland transport of supplies and personnel to force the other three countries out of Berlin.

The United States countered with a massive airlift, flying airplanes into Berlin around the clock loaded with food, fuel, and other goods. The supplies, some ten thousand tons a day, were needed for the 2 million people living in the three Western zones of occupation.

Beaten by the airlift, the Soviet Union ended the blockade in May 1949. By the end of the year the opposing powers had created two sep-

arate German nations—the Federal Republic of Germany, a liberal democracy aligned with the West, and the German Democratic Republic, ruled by the Soviets. The two nations were more simply known as West Germany and East Germany. The division continued until 1990 when Germany was finally reunited.

A Fateful Year

The lines between cold war participants became fixed in 1949 with the founding of the North Atlantic Treaty Organization (NATO). The United States, Canada, and ten Western European nations formed the military alliance to resist Soviet aggression. NATO members pledged that an

Foreign and defense ministers from Great Britain, France, and the United States meet to discuss formation of the North Atlantic Treaty Organization (NATO). NATO is a military organization that aligned the United States and Western European nations against the Soviet Union and its satellites.

armed attack on any of the nations would be considered an attack on all of them. It was the first time the United States had entered into such an alliance.

The Soviet Union responded by creating the Warsaw Pact, with Eastern European nations under its domination as members. It also tried to bolster the economies of its Eastern bloc satellite nations the same way the United States was trying to strengthen European nations. But over the next few decades the Soviet bloc economies lagged behind those of Western nations, contributing to unrest in these countries and to communism's eventual failure.

The year 1949 was also important in the cold war for two Communist successes, the takeover of China and the Soviet Union's first successful explosion of an atomic bomb.

The United States had poured billions of dollars into China to keep the Nationalists in power, but the Communists under Mao Tse-tung proved too strong. They won the four-year civil war and the Nationalist government fled to Taiwan, an island possession of China. The establishment of a Communist regime in the world's most populous nation was a severe blow to the United States and raised fears that other Asian countries would also embrace communism. U.S. efforts to prevent further Communist expansion, fueled by the policy of containment first articulated by Kennan, led to U.S. involvement in the Korean War in 1950 and the Vietnam War in the '60s and '70s.

In September 1949 the United States received another piece of devastating news—the Soviet Union had successfully tested an atomic bomb. Public fear of the Soviet Union increased in the United States, and the new Soviet capability led Truman to order the development of the H-bomb (hydrogen bomb); the first H-bomb, exploded in 1952, was eight hundred times more powerful than the atomic bomb dropped over Hiroshima.

The result was an arms race in which the two nations vied, at tremendous cost, to produce bigger and more deadly bombs, missile systems, and other weapons

The Hollywood Ten

In 1947 the House Un-American Activities Committee (HUAC) began conducting, closed-door hearings to investigate allegations of communism in the movie industry.

One of HUAC's complaints was that Hollywood had produced pro-Russian films such as *Mission to Moscow*, *North Star*, and *Song of Russia*. HUAC ignored the fact that the films had been made at the urging of the Office of War Information, which wanted Americans to sympathize with their new ally.

The committee interviewed actors like Robert Taylor, Ronald Reagan, and Gary Cooper and studio owners such as Walt Disney. Some witnesses testified to alleged subversive activities and named names of alleged communists.

But ten witnesses, all screenwriters, refused to answer questions, including whether they had ever been a member of the Communist Party. Cited for contempt of Congress, the Hollywood Ten, as they were called, all served one year in a federal prison in Danbury, Connecticut. Another inmate at the time was J. Parnell Thomas, a former HUAC chairman who had been convicted of illegally placing people on his congressional payroll and pocketing their salaries.

The ten were blacklisted after their release. This meant their names were put on lists of workers studios would not hire. The blacklist went unchallenged until 1960 when Dalton Trumbo worked openly and received credit for his work on the films *Exodus* and *Spartacus*.

A mushroom cloud climbs into the sky in 1946 after the United States deto-nates an atomic bomb at Bikini Atoll in the South Pacific.

in the quest for military superiority. Albert Einstein, who played a significant role in developing the atomic bomb, wrote: "The armament race between the USA and USSR, originally supposed to be a preventive measure, assumes hysterical character. On both sides the means to mass destruction are perfected with feverish haste. . . . In the end, there beckons more and more clearly general annihilation." [48]

The only positive effect of the arms race was the deterrent effect of knowing that a nuclear strike by one superpower would mean nuclear retaliation from the other. The fear on both sides of the devastating effects of nuclear war created a stalemate that, almost by itself, kept the weapons from being used.

Fear of Nuclear War

Although neither side in the cold war would ever use nuclear weapons, the threat of nuclear war was very real to Americans by the end of the decade. Many people believed World War III, a final conflict between the United States and the Soviets, was inevitable. They worried it could lead to a nuclear holocaust.

The feeling of safety that followed hard-won victory in World War II was fleeting. Although Americans had rejoiced over development of the atomic bomb because it ended the war, they began to fear it as they learned more about its awesome power. In its August 8, 1945, edition, the daily *Milwaukee Journal* published a large map of the city. Overlaid on the map were rings that showed the range of devastation if the city were hit with a nuclear bomb. Other newspapers and magazines wrote accounts of future nuclear wars that could wipe out all life on the planet or leave Earth a shattered hulk, with only pockets of civilization surviving.

The Cold War Legacy

The first few years of the cold war in the '40s left a legacy of paranoia and fear of the Soviet Union that peaked in the next decade when people dug home-made bomb shelters, children started wearing civil defense bracelets so their bodies could be identified in case of nuclear attack, and foreign policy had a single focus—stopping the advance of communism around the world.

The threat of nuclear holocaust added an emotional base of fear to the ideological conflict. This emotion all too often swept away common sense in dealings between the two nations. As one historian wrote: "The vulnerability to weapons that could destroy entire countries . . . heightened fears and antagonisms and made the struggle for power and influence appear to be also a struggle for survival."[49]

The cold war was a struggle that would shape America's future for the next fifty years.

Epilogue

This young couple and their baby stride boldly into the future, as did the United States at the end of the forties. The tumultuous decade created great changes in America and raised the hopes of its citizens for a better life in the years to come.

The forties was a pivotal decade of the twentieth century and one of the most important in U.S. history. It was a period of transition, of crisis for the nation and for its citizens.

The United States emerged from World War II as a superpower, the strongest nation in the world militarily, economically, and politically. Its ailing economy healed by war spending, the United States began the longest period of continued economic growth in its history. Its citizens were having babies and buying homes and cars in record numbers as they reveled in peacetime prosperity.

The war itself had created a huge redistribution of wealth that fueled significant growth in the nation's middle class.

In 1939 the top 5 percent of earners controlled 23 percent of the disposable income. By 1945 that figure had dropped to 17 percent, which meant significantly more people had spending money in their pockets. This was due to wartime tax policies, the success of labor unions, and programs such as Social Security that shifted wealth to people who traditionally

President Franklin D. Roosevelt (seated in the middle and surrounded by his cabinet) was one of the strongest presidents in U.S. history. His imaginative, forceful use of the powers of the executive branch expanded the traditional role of the presidency and left it a more powerful position than ever before.

had not had much money.

The GI Bill played a significant part in the nation's new lifestyle by allowing millions to buy homes for the first time, start their own businesses, and attend college. By 1947, when GI enrollment peaked, servicemen accounted for more than 1 million of the nation's 2.5 million college students. Many people who before the war could only dream of higher education were able to become doctors, lawyers, scientists, and teachers. They swelled the ranks of the growing middle class and led the march to the suburbs.

Some of the GIs taking advantage

of those benefits were women. American women had won a new sense of freedom and accomplishment by fighting for their country and working for victory in factories. More women than ever before continued working after the war. They forged their way into new professions and jobs from which they were traditionally excluded.

Postwar demand for new homes led to a mass migration to the suburbs. The explosion of new communities ringing large cities would continue for several decades. This movement even changed the nation's economic structure as factories and businesses relocated to the suburbs.

The Japanese bombs that sank ships and shattered U.S. spirits also destroyed the country's traditional policy of isolationism, spurring the nation to take a central role on the world stage.

"We have learned that we cannot live alone, at peace; that our well-being is dependent on the well-being of other nations, far away. We have learned to be citizens of the world, members of the community," [50] said President Franklin D. Roosevelt on January 20, 1945, in his fourth inaugural speech.

Superpower Status

America's status as a superpower brought new responsibilities to a nation that was unaccustomed to playing a continuing role in world affairs. But President Harry Truman and Congress, many of whose members had wanted nothing to do with foreign countries before Pearl Harbor, quickly learned how to wield this new power.

The United States, which in the past had kept its distance from the problems of the world, accepted the burden of helping other nations recover from the war. The United States also assumed the leading role in the fight against the new totalitarian threat of communism.

The decade also saw the continued growth of the power of the presidency. Before Roosevelt's election in 1932, Congress had more overall authority in setting policy and running the country. But by taking charge in an economic emergency, Roosevelt greatly expanded the role and power of the executive branch. During World War II he wielded even greater control over the nation.

The result of his twelve years in office was a shift in the basic balance of power between the executive and legislative branches of federal government. The president now had the upper hand in setting both domestic and foreign policy.

The stature of the office also increased because the nation had become a world power. The president was called the head of "the strongest nation in the world" and the "leader of the free world." When the president spoke other nations listened and usually concurred.

America would never be the same again. The Japanese bombs at Pearl Harbor had not only destroyed American ships, they had ended an era. They had given the nation a new role to play in world events and changed the future of every man, woman, and child in America.

Notes

Introduction

1. Quoted in James West Davidson et al., *Nation of Nations: A Narrative History of the American Republic.* 2nd ed. New York: McGraw-Hill, 1994, p. 960.
2. Quoted in Joseph Alsop, *FDR: A Centenary Remembrance.* New York: Viking, 1982, p. 115.

Chapter One:
America Enters the War

3. Quoted in Henry Steele Commager, *Living Ideas in America.* New York: Harper & Row, 1964, p. 655.
4. Quoted in C. L. Sulzberger, *American Heritage Picture History of World War II.* New York: American Heritage, 1966, p. 130.
5. Quoted in Cabell Phillips, *The 1940s: Decade of Triumph and Trouble.* New York: Macmillan, 1975, p. 141.
6. Quoted in Thomas A. Bailey and David M. Kennedy, *The American Pageant.* 8th ed. Lexington, MA: D. C. Heath, 1987, p. 786.
7. Quoted in Phillips, *The 1940s,* p. 64.
8. Quoted in Sulzberger, *American Heritage Picture History of World War II,* p. 149.
9. Quoted in Ronald H. Bailey, *The Home Front: U.S.A.* Alexandria, VA: Time-Life Books, 1977, p.12.
10. Quoted in Bailey, *The Home Front,* p. 12.
11. Quoted in Ralph G. Martin, *The GI War.* Boston: Little, Brown, 1973, p. 11.

Chapter Two: America at War:
The Home Front

12. Quoted in Paul D. Casdorph, *Let the Good Times Roll: Life at Home in America During WWII.* New York: Paragon House, 1989, p. 3.
13. Quoted in John Morton Blum, *V Was for Victory.* New York: Harcourt Brace Jovanovich, 1976, p. 95.
14. Quoted in Deb Mulvey, ed., *"We Pulled Together . . . and Won!"* Greendale, WI: Reminisce Books, 1993, p. 58.
15. Quoted in Phillips, *The 1940s,* p. 107.
16. Quoted in Warren G. Harris, *Gable & Lombard.* New York: Simon & Schuster, 1974, p. 149.
17. Quoted in Mulvey, *"We Pulled Together . . . and Won!",* p. 42.

Chapter Three: Winning the War

18. Quoted in Casdorph, *Let the Good Times Roll,* p. 30.
19. Quoted in John J. Vail, *World War II: The War in Europe.* San Diego: Lucent Books, 1991, p. 57.
20. Quoted in Phillips, *The 1940s,* p. 270.

Chapter Four:
The Movies Go to War

21. Quoted in Ezra Bowen, ed., *This Fabulous Century 1940–1950.* New York: Time-Life Books, 1969, p. 184.
22. Quoted in Clayton B. Koppes and Gregory D. Black, *Hollywood Goes to War.* New York: Free Press, 1987, p. 64.
23. Quoted in Joe Morella, Edward Z. Epstein, and John Griggs, *The Films of World War II.* Spartacus, NJ: Citadel Press, 1980, p. 77.
24. Quoted in Koppes and Black, *Hollywood Goes to War,* p. 66.
25. Quoted in Koppes and Black, *Hollywood Goes to War,* p. 65.
26. Quoted in Koppes and Black, *Hollywood Goes to War,* p. 98.
27. Quoted in Koppes and Black, *Hollywood Goes to War,* p. 260.
28. Quoted in John Belton, *American Cinema/American Culture.* New York: McGraw-Hill, 1994, pp. 30, 31.

29. Quoted in Morella, Epstein, and Griggs, *The Films of World War II,* p. 133.
30. Quoted in Koppes and Black, *Hollywood Goes to War,* p. 185.
31. Quoted in Morella, Epstein, and Griggs, *The Films of World War II,* p. 57.
32. Quoted in Jules B. Billard, ed., *We Americans.* Washington, DC: National Geographic Society, 1975, p. 376.

Chapter Five: Postwar Life

33. Quoted in Charles Panati, *Panati's Parade of Fads, Follies, and Manias.* New York: HarperPerennial, 1991, p. 217.
34. Quoted in D. Duane Cummins and William Gee White, *Combat and Consensus: The 1940's and 1950's.* Encino, CA: Glencoe, 1972, p. 192.
35. Quoted in Casdorph, *Let the Good Times Roll,* p. 111.

Chapter Six: Popular Culture:
From Jack Benny to Howdy Doody

36. Quoted in Robert Campbell, *The Golden Years of Broadcasting.* New York: Charles Scribner's Sons, 1976, p. 99.
37. Quoted in Casdorph, *Let the Good Times Roll,* p. 148.
38: Quoted in Harry Castleman and Walter J. Podrazik, *Watching TV:*

Four Decades of American Television. New York: McGraw-Hill, 1982, p. 30.

39. Quoted in Daniel Okrent and Harris Lewine, eds., *The Ultimate Baseball Book.* Boston: Houghton Mifflin, 1979, p. 211.

40. Quoted in Ben Olan, ed., *Pursuit of Excellence: The Olympic Story.* Danbury, CT: Grolier, 1983, p. 150.

Chapter Seven: The Cold War

41. Quoted in Robert Poley, ed., *The Truman Years: The Words and Times of Harry S. Truman.* Waukesha, WI: Country Beautiful, 1976, p. 69.

42. Quoted in Martin Walker, *The Cold War: A History.* New York: Henry Holt, 1993, p. 41.

43. Quoted in Walker, *The Cold War,* p. 42.

44. Quoted in Walker, *The Cold War,* p. 37.

45. Quoted in Commager, *Living Ideas in America,* p. 722.

46. Quoted in Phillips, *The 1940s,* p. 306.

47. Quoted in Walker, *The Cold War,* p. 66.

48. Quoted in Samuel Eliot Morison, Henry Steele Commager, and William E. Leuchtenburg, *The Growth of the American Republic.* 6th ed. Vol. 2. New York: Oxford University Press, 1969, p. 635.

49. Thomas B. Larson, *Soviet-American Rivalry.* New York: Norton, 1978, p. 4.

Epilogue

50. Quoted in Phillips, *The 1940s,* p. 243.

Chronology

1939

September 1: German troops invade Poland; two days later Great Britain, France, Australia, and New Zealand declare war on Germany.

September 17: Soviet Union invades Poland from the east.

November 4: Congress approves "cash-and-carry" clause in Neutrality Act to allow Great Britain and France to buy arms.

1940

January 3: President Franklin D. Roosevelt calls for $1.8 billion in defense appropriations.

April 9: Germany invades Denmark and Norway.

May 10: Germany invades the Netherlands, Belgium, and Luxembourg; within days German troops push into northern France.

May 31: Roosevelt tells Congress the United States should be building fifty thousand airplanes annually; he calls for $1.3 billion in supplemental funds for military and naval development.

June 22: France surrenders.

July 10: Battle of Britain begins.

Sept. 7: London Blitz begins.

September 16: Roosevelt signs the Selective Service Training and Service Act requiring males age twenty and older to register for the military draft.

November 5: Roosevelt is reelected to a third term.

December 20: The Office of Production Management is established to regulate defense production and facilitate shipment of war matériel to Allied nations.

1941

January 8: Roosevelt proposes a record budget of $17.5 billion, almost 60 percent committed to defense spending.

March 11–12: Congress passes the Lend-Lease Act, which provides supplies to nations fighting the Axis powers.

April 11: Roosevelt creates the Office of Price Administration to plan wage and price controls.

May 27: Roosevelt declares unlimited state of emergency.

June 24: Roosevelt issues $40 million in credits to the Soviet Union two days after the German invasion begins.

July 25: Roosevelt embargoes shipments of scrap iron and gasoline to Japan and freezes all Japanese assets in the United States.

August 9–12: Roosevelt and British prime minister Winston Churchill meet off Newfoundland to sign the Atlantic Charter.

December 7: Japanese attack Pearl Harbor.

December 8: Calling the attack on Pearl Harbor "a date which will live in infamy," Roosevelt asks a joint session of Congress to declare war on Japan; Congress approves the declaration.

December 11: Germany and Italy declare war on the United States.

1942

January 2: Manila falls to Japan, causing Gen. Douglas MacArthur and American and Philippine troops to withdraw to Bataan, a small peninsula opposite Manila.

March: The U.S. government forces 110,000 Americans of Japanese ancestry living in California into remote internment camps.

March 17: General MacArthur withdraws to Australia in the face of advancing Japanese forces.

April 18: The War Manpower Commission is set up to maximize the effective use of available workers; bombers take off from the aircraft carrier USS *Hornet* and fly 650 miles to bomb Tokyo and other cities in the first U.S. attack against Japan.

May 4–8: In the Battle of the Coral Sea, U.S. naval and air forces intercept a Japanese fleet between Australia and the Solomon Islands.

May 12: First mass execution of Jews by gas at Auschwitz.

June 4–6: The Battle of Midway.

July 22: The United States issues gasoline rationing coupons.

August 17: United States bombers make their first raid on Europe.

November 8: A combined army of 400,000 U.S. and British soldiers led by Gen. Dwight D. Eisenhower lands in Morocco and Algeria to fight Axis powers.

December 2: First atomic reaction achieved in Chicago.

December 4: The Works Progress Administration is closed.

1943

January 12–24: Roosevelt meets with Churchill and chief military advisers in Casablanca, Morocco, to plan Allied strategy.

April 8: Roosevelt freezes all wages, salaries, and prices.

May 27: Roosevelt forbids racial discrimination in any industry accepting government war contracts.

June 20: Detroit race riot begins, one of several that hit major cities through the summer.

July 10–August 17: Allied forces invade Sicily.

September 9: British and U.S. forces land at Salerno.

November 9: Representatives of forty- four nations meet in Washington to establish the United Nations Relief and Rehabilitation Administration to provide help for war victims.

November 28–December 1: Roosevelt, Churchill, and Soviet premier Joseph Stalin meet in Tehran, Iran, and pledge their cooperation in the war effort.

1944

January 31: U.S. troops capture three of the Marshall Islands; by February 22 they control entire chain of islands in the Pacific.

February 29: The Office of Price Administration says the U.S. black market is worth $1 billion a year.

June 6: D day; Allies cross the English Channel in Operation Overlord, the greatest military invasion in history. Before the day is over, seventy thousand Americans will land on Utah and Omaha Beaches on the Normandy coast while eighty-three thousand Allied troops establish footholds on beaches east of the U.S. position.

June 13: Germans launch the first V-1 rockets against London; the V-1, nicknamed the "buzz bomb," is a jet-propelled missile that flies at 350 miles per hour and carries a ton of explosives.

June 22: Roosevelt signs the Servicemen's Readjustment Act, known as the GI Bill.

July 21–August 10: U.S. forces capture Guam.

August 21–September 21: Groundwork is laid for the United Nations at the Dumbarton Oaks Conference in Washington, D.C.

August 25: Allied troops liberate Paris from four years of German occupation.

November 7: Roosevelt is reelected to a fourth term.

November 24: All-out air attacks begin on Tokyo from the Marianas, a chain of islands in the Pacific; previously, air raids had been launched from ships.

December 16–26: The Battle of the Bulge.

1945

January 2: Americans of Japanese ancestry are no longer excluded from the West Coast.

January 9: General MacArthur's

troops land on Luzon, the main island of the Philippines.

February 4–12: The Big Three—Roosevelt, Churchill, and Stalin—meet at Yalta in the Crimea.

February 19–March 16: U.S. troops capture Iwo Jima in one of the fiercest battles of the war; the importance of the island is that it is only 750 miles from Tokyo, which means all of Japan is now in range of medium-range bombers.

March 7: U.S. troops cross the Rhine River at Remagen to enter Germany.

April 1–July 2: Okinawa is captured, giving the Allies a land base from which to attack Japan.

April 12: Roosevelt dies at Warm Springs, Georgia. Vice President Harry S Truman becomes president.

April 15–June 26: Representatives of fifty nations meet in San Francisco to draft the charter for the United Nations; the document is signed on June 26.

April 30: Adolf Hitler commits suicide.

May 7: Germany surrenders.

July 16: The first atomic bomb is detonated near Alamogordo, New Mexico.

August 6: The *Enola Gay*, a B-29 bomber, drops an atomic bomb on Hiroshima.

August 9: A second atomic bomb is dropped on Nagasaki.

August 14: The Japanese government surrenders; War Manpower Commission relinquishes control of the nation's workers.

August 18: Truman orders full restoration of consumer products and a free market economy.

September 2: The formal surrender of Japan occurs aboard the battleship *Missouri* in Tokyo harbor.

October 24: The United Nations charter is activated.

November 20: War crimes trials open in Nuremberg, Germany.

1946

March 5: Former prime minister Winston Churchill coins the term "iron curtain" to describe the political barrier around Eastern European countries that have come under communist control.

May 3: War crimes trials open in Tokyo.

July 4: The Philippine Islands are given full independence from the United States in a ceremony in Manila.

August 1: Truman signs the bill creating the Atomic Energy Commission, which will have regulatory powers over the production and use of nuclear energy.

November 5: Republicans capture control of both the House and Senate in congressional elections.

1947

February 10: Peace treaties are signed in Paris between Allied nations and five of the Axis powers (Bulgaria, Romania, Hungary, Italy, and Finland), but no settlement has been reached with Germany.

March 12: Truman formulates a doctrine of aiding noncommunist nations that seek assistance against communist takeover.

March 22: Truman announces a program to check the loyalty of all U.S. government workers.

June 5: George C. Marshall proposes a plan to assist European economic recovery, thereafter known as the Marshall Plan.

June 11: The last World War II rationing program, for sugar, comes to an end.

June 23: Taft-Hartley Act, which reduces the power of labor unions, is passed over Truman's veto.

1948

April 3: Truman signs the Economic Cooperation Act, which will fund the Marshall Plan. The bill provides $5.6 billion for sixteen countries in fifteen months; additional funds are allocated for military and economic aid to Greece, Turkey, and China.

April 30: The Organization of American States is formed; representatives from twenty-one Western Hemisphere nations sign a charter that outlaws the intervention of one state into the internal affairs of another.

May 31–June 7: The United States, Great Britain, France, and the Benelux countries agree to set up a West German state divided into three military zones.

June 11: Sugar rationing ends.

June 21–26: The Soviet Union begins a land and water blockade of Berlin, prompting an airlift by U.S. and British forces; the blockade is not broken until May 1949.

June 24: The Selective Service System is reactivated; all men ages eighteen to twenty-five must register and, at age nineteen, can be called up to serve for up to twenty-one months. A peacetime force of just over 2 million is authorized.

July 17: Democrats who oppose Truman for president meet in Birmingham, Alabama, and form the States Right Party. Governor Strom Thurmond of South Carolina is nominated for president and Fielding Wright for vice president.

November 2: Truman defeats Thomas

Dewey to win a four-year term as president.

1949

January 20: Truman sworn in as the thirty-third president.

February 24: An altitude record for rockets is set when a small rocket flies 250 miles above its launch site at White Sands, New Mexico.

April 4: The North Atlantic Treaty Organization is formed to meet the rising threat of aggression from the Soviet Union. Its twelve member nations, including the United States, meet in Washington to establish terms for their mutual defense.

September 3: The United States learns the Soviet Union has developed an atomic bomb; until now, the United States was the only nuclear power.

October 1–November 11: Steelworkers strike nationwide over the issue of pensions. Bethlehem Steel is the first company to settle, promising to pay workers $100 a month at age sixty-five after twenty-five years of service.

October 24: Permanent UN headquarters in New York is dedicated.

October 26: The minimum wage is raised from 40 to 75 cents an hour.

November 7: General Motors announces a record profit of $500 million for the first nine months of the year.

December: Communists led by Mao Tse-tung win control of mainland China; Nationalist government of Chiang Kai-shek flees to Taiwan.

For Further Reading

Jules B. Billard, ed., *We Americans.* Washington, DC: National Geographic Society, 1975.

Jacqueline Farrell, *The Great Depression.* San Diego: Lucent Books, 1996.

Kathleen Krull, *V Is for Victory.* New York: Knopf, 1995.

Calvin D. Linton, ed., *The Bicentennial Almanac.* New York: Thomas Nelson, 1975.

Charles Panati, *Panati's Parade of Fads, Follies, and Manias.* New York: HarperPerennial, 1991.

George Sullivan, *The Day Pearl Harbor Was Bombed: A Photo History of World War II.* New York: Scholastic, 1991.

C. L. Sulzberger, *American Heritage Picture History of World War II.* New York: American Heritage, 1966.

John J. Vail, *World War II: The War in Europe.* San Diego: Lucent Books, 1991.

Works Consulted

Joseph Alsop, *FDR: A Centenary Remembrance.* New York: Viking, 1982.

Ronald H. Bailey, *The Home Front: U.S.A.* Alexandria, VA: Time-Life Books, 1977.

Thomas A. Bailey and David M. Kennedy, *The American Pageant.* 8th ed. Lexington, MA: D. C. Heath, 1987.

Alan G. Barbour, *Cliffhanger: A Pictorial History of the Motion Picture Serial.* Secaucus, NJ: Citadel Press, 1977.

Stephen Becker, *Comic Art in America.* New York: Simon & Schuster, 1959.

John Belton, *American Cinema/American Culture.* New York: McGraw-Hill, 1994.

Marcia Blitz, *Donald Duck.* New York: Crown, 1979.

John Morton Blum, *V Was for Victory.* New York: Harcourt Brace Jovanovich, 1976.

Ezra Bowen, ed., *This Fabulous*

Century 1940–1950. New York: Time-Life Books, 1969.

Robert Campbell, *The Golden Years of Broadcasting*. New York: Charles Scribner's Sons, 1976.

Paul D. Casdorph, *Let the Good Times Roll: Life at Home in America During WWII*. New York: Paragon House, 1989.

Harry Castleman and Walter J. Podrazik. *Watching TV: Four Decades of American Television*. New York: McGraw-Hill, 1982.

Thurston Clarke, *Pearl Harbor Ghosts*. New York: William Morrow, 1991.

Henry Steele Commager, *Living Ideas in America*. New York: Harper & Row, 1964.

D. Duane Cummins and William Gee White, *Combat and Consensus: The 1940's and 1950's*. Encino, CA: Glencoe, 1972.

Les Daniels, *Marvel: Five Fabulous Decades of the World's Greatest Comics*. Hong Kong: Abradale Press, 1991.

James West Davidson et al., *Nation of Nations: A Narrative History of the American Republic*. 2nd ed. New York: McGraw-Hill, 1994.

Phillip T. Drotning, *Black Heroes in Our Nation's History*. New York: Cowles, 1969.

Norman H. Finkelstein, *Sounds in the Air: The Golden Age of Radio*. New York: Charles Scribner's Sons, 1993.

Donald M. Goldstein, Katherine V. Dillon, and J. Michael Wenger, *The Way It Was: Pearl Harbor*. Washington, DC: Brassey's, 1991.

Warren G. Harris, *Gable & Lombard*. New York: Simon & Schuster, 1974.

Karla Jennings, *The Devouring Fungus*. New York: W.W. Norton, 1990.

Howard Koch, *Casablanca: Spirit and Legend*. Woodstock, NY: Overlook Press, 1973.

Clayton B. Koppes and Gregory D. Black, *Hollywood Goes to War*. New York: Free Press, 1987.

Thomas B. Larson, *Soviet-American Rivalry*. New York: Norton, 1978.

John Margolies and Emily Gwathmey, *Ticket to Paradise: American Movie Theaters and How We Had Fun*. Boston: Little, Brown, 1991.

Rick Marschall, *The History of Television*. New York: Gallery Books, 1986.

Ralph G. Martin, *The GI War*. Boston: Little, Brown, 1973.

George R. Metcalf, *Black Profiles*. New York: McGraw-Hill, 1970.

Joe Morella, Edward Z. Epstein, and John Griggs, *The Films of World War II*. Spartacus, NJ: Citadel Press, 1980.

Samuel Eliot Morison, Henry Steele Commager, and William E.

Leuchtenburg, *The Growth of the American Republic*. 6th ed.Vol. 2. New York: Oxford University Press, 1969.

Deb Mulvey, ed., *"We Pulled Together. . . . and Won!"* Greendale, WI: Reminisce Books, 1993.

David Nichols, *Ernie's War: The Best of Ernie Pyle's World War II Dispatches*. New York: Simon & Schuster, 1987.

Ben Olan, ed., *Pursuit of Excellence: The Olympic Story*. Danbury, CT: Grolier, 1983.

Daniel Okrent and Harris Lewine, eds., *The Ultimate Baseball Book*. Boston: Houghton Mifflin, 1979.

Charles Panati, *Panati's Parade of Fads, Follies, and Manias*. New York: HarperPerennial, 1991.

Joseph E. Persico, *Edward R. Murrow: An American Original*. New York: McGraw-Hill, 1988.

Cabell Phillips, *The 1940s: Decade of Triumph and Trouble*. New York: Macmillan, 1975.

Richard Polenberg, ed., *America at War: The Home Front 1941–45*. Englewood Cliffs, NJ: Prentice-Hall, 1968.

Robert Poley, ed., *The Truman Years: The Words and Times of Harry S. Truman*. Waukesha, WI: Country Beautiful, 1976.

Donald I. Rogers, *Since You Went Away*. New Rochelle, NY: Arlington House, 1973.

Glenhall Taylor, *Before Television*. New York: A. S. Barnes, 1979.

John Russell Taylor, *Hollywood 1940s*. New York: Gallery Books, 1985.

Martin Walker, *The Cold War: A History*. New York: Henry Holt, 1993.

Doris Weatherford, *American Women and World War II*. New York: Facts On File, 1990.

Index

Picture Credits

About the Author

Michael V. Uschan is the author of *A Multicultural Portrait of World War I* and *A Basic Guide to Luge*, part of a series written for the U.S. Olympic Committee. Mr. Uschan began his career as a writer and editor with United Press International, a wire service that provided news reports to newspapers and radio and television stations. Noting that journalism is sometimes called "history in a hurry," he considers writing history books a natural extension of the skills he developed as a journalist. He lives with his wife, Barbara, in Franklin, Wisconsin, a suburb of Milwaukee.